FROM *CHARIOTS OF FIRE*
TO *THE KING'S SPEECH*

From *Chariots of Fire* to *The King's Speech*

Writing Biopics and Docudramas

Alan Rosenthal

Southern Illinois University Press • *Carbondale*

17 16 15 14   4 3 2 1

Library of Congress Cataloging-in-Publication Data
Rosenthal, Alan.
From Chariots of fire to The king's speech : writing biopics and
docudramas / Alan Rosenthal.
    p. cm.
Includes bibliographical references and index.
    ISBN 978-0-8093-3298-4 (pbk. : alk. paper)
    ISBN 0-8093-3298-1 (pbk. : alk. paper)
    ISBN 978-0-8093-3299-1 (ebook)
    ISBN 0-8093-3299-X (ebook)
1. Motion picture authorship. 2. Biographical drama—Authorship.
3. Historical drama—Authorship. I. Title.
PN1996.R68 2013
808.23—dc23   2013022182

Printed on recycled paper. ♻

The paper used in this publication meets the minimum requirements of
American National Standard for Information Sciences—Permanence of
Paper for Printed Library Materials, ANSI Z39.48-1992. ∞

For
Bobby Cramer

*for your wonderful and generous support
over so many years*

CONTENTS

PREFACE

When David Seidler took to the stage in 2011, to receive the best screenplay Academy Award for *The King's Speech*, he must have been a very happy man. He was seventy-three years old. The idea for the film had been with him for years, and now his efforts were crowned with the small golden statuette in his hand. Seventy-one years before, his work might have been admired, but there would have been no statue, as the Academy Award for original screenplay was instituted only in 1940.

The lack of recognition of the writer's place was typical of that age. When the Academy Awards were instituted, the feted names were those of the actors and the producers. The writer, if and when acknowledged, was placed very low on the totem pole of the Hollywood hierarchy. Though directors were valued, the producer was king.

Times change. By the time I first took up film, all I heard about was the "auteur theory."

This was the decade of the director, who was not only king but God as well. Because of the efforts of young, vociferous film critics, the producer was being pushed aside. Slowly and reluctantly, the industry had to admit that other talents were necessary in filmmaking besides financial acumen and organization.

Today, however, I would like to think we've entered the age of the writer (even though realistically I know special effects rule the roost). Finally, the writer is getting not just the proper financial rewards that are his or her due (but only after endless writers' strikes) but also the recognition that without a good script there is no film.

There is also the recognition that scriptwriting is a demanding occupation. Unlike many other film professionals, as a writer, you cannot bluff your way through. Hence the low enrollment for scriptwriting in many film schools. In such a course, you really have to work and prove yourself. While many a director has been saved by his director of photography, or by a creative editor, the writer stands—or should I say sits—alone. It's a daunting prospect but also an exhilarating one.

How can a textbook like this help you get going as a writer? By offering you two things: maps and tools. Maps show you the terrain, the difficulties, the obstacles, and the problems you face. The tools, consisting of techniques, hints, script analysis, and suggestions, show you how to overcome the problems. Whether you get to the end of your journey successfully obviously also depends on your talent, luck, drive, and energy; but with this book as your guide, you should have a great send-off.

However, the fact-based script, or docudrama, path is like no other. You are entering strange terrain, trodden before and yet still waiting to be explored. It's a peculiar landscape where real people's lives, actual tragedies, the shadows of history, and the devastations, furies, and comedies of the present keep begging you to tell their strange stories as you proceed on your way.

If fictional drama is represented by the familiar lowlands and valleys, docudrama can be seen as the mysterious cloud-hidden mountains and peaks. A rough map of the area is given in chapter 3, but a lot is still booby-trapped territory.

Do you need specialized skills for this kind of venture? Well, there's the beauty. Provided you have some essential basic talent, you can write good docudrama; that is, if you are willing to put in the training, look at the maps, observe the techniques, and listen to others who have gone before. Though writing the fact-based film parallels in many respects the writing of other forms of drama, it is also, as suggested above, tremendously different. How you cope with the differences is one of the major concerns of this book.

Beyond techniques, attitudes to truth, and responsibilities to audience, one other thing appears to me to differentiate docudrama from fictional drama: the mindset of many of the writers. Some of them see docudrama as just a specialized branch of drama, whose sole purpose is to entertain while using fact-based material. However, many other writers working in the genre see their work as especially socially challenging. While they too want to entertain and provide pleasure to the viewer, they also want to provoke their audience, to present hard questions, and occasionally to change the current scene. I like to consider myself part of this second group, which accounts for a lot of the subtext of this book.

However, the journey is yours. If your technique and craftsmanship are good—and those are the things that this book will give you—and if you've got drive and energy, then there is nothing that can match scriptwriting. So good luck on the trip.

ACKNOWLEDGMENTS

First, my thanks to all those people and organizations who let me look at their films and burrow through their scripts. In particular, I would like to thank Ruth Caleb of the BBC, Ian McBride of Granada TV, and Brian Siberell of HBO; they all gave me immense help and made this book possible. I would also like to thank Henry Breitrose, David Elstein, Peter Goodchild, and George Stoney, who helped me tie up some loose ends.

I also have an immense debt of gratitude to scriptwriters Michael Baker, Stephen Davis, Gerald Green, Ernest Kinoy, Robert Loiderman, Peter Prince, Antony Thomas, and Fletcher Watkins. All of them took time to talk to me, show me their work, discuss the intricacies of docudrama, and allow me to quote freely from their scripts. They showed me how it could be done.

I am also grateful to the following stations, producers, organizations, and authors, who provided me with different materials and allowed me to produce extracts from their documents or scripts: the BBC; CBS; Joe Cacaci; Bob Cooper; Granada TV; Home Box Office (HBO); David Hodgson; Andrew Morton; NBC; the National Film Board of Canada; Patchett-Kaufmann Entertainment; Thames TV; Martin Poll; University of California Press; the Writers Guild of America; and Stephen Zito. Along with thanks, I would also like to acknowledge that all the script or document extracts used retain the copyright of the original owners.

Many friends assisted me with this book over and above the call of duty. Ben and Melinda Levin, together with Don Staples, showed me Texas hospitality and pointed me in the right direction. Harrison Engle toiled tirelessly in Los Angeles, tracking down writers and getting me script permissions. And my beloved friend Bobby Cramer, who has provided life support and humor for so many years for me in New York, dropped everything to get me the latest and most up-to-date docudrama scripts around.

Four people who had a very strong influence on me while writing the book were Leslie Woodhead and Michael Eaton, and Robert Freedman and Shaun Miller.

As head of docudrama at Granada TV, Leslie was the person really responsible for introducing me to the subject of docudrama many, many years ago. Since then, we have had dozens of talks, worth more to me than gold.

Michael Eaton, for his part, is a prince among writers and has spent endless hours showing me how to develop a good script. Both Michael and Leslie advised me on the writing of *The First Fagin*, and again I admit a deep debt to the both of them.

Robert Freedman, another old friend, is a New York lawyer and possibly the top American authority on film finance and distribution contracts. Shaun Miller is also a top media lawyer, working in Melbourne, Australia, whose friendship and hospitality sustained me while I was making a docudrama Down Under. With infinite patience, both Robert and Shaun guided me through the complex world of film legalities. In chapter 12, the wisdom is Bob's and Shaun's, the mistakes mine. My thanks to Bob and Shaun for everything.

Unbounded thanks also to George Custen. Professor Custen's book *Biopics* was a treasure chest of information constantly by my side. Similarly, I found immense help delving into the books on docudrama by Derek Paget and Steve Lipkin. Both are the two most acknowledged academic experts in the field, with whom I've had the luck to become good friends. They, above anyone else, brought me up to date on what's happening in the fields.

Finally thanks to my wife, Tirtza, and my editor Karl Kageff. Tirtza offered suggestions, cake, coffee, wine, and moral support when these things were most needed. My last guiding light was my editor Karl Kageff, who provided excellent advice and tremendous enthusiasm every inch of the way. Tirtza and Karl made a great support team. I doff my hat to both of you.

From *Chariots of Fire* to *The King's Speech*

INTRODUCTION

Early in 2011, the two most important candidates for the Oscar for best film of the year were *The King's Speech* and *The Social Network*. In the end, *The King's Speech* took the award not only for best film but also for best script. Two years earlier, the film *Milk*, about gay rights activist Harvey Milk, was nominated for eight Oscars and won for best actor and best original screenplay. In 2013, again the Oscar for best film went to a docudrama, *Argo*, about the rescue of Americans in Iran.

What was interesting was that *The King's Speech*, *Milk*, and *Argo* were films based on real people and real historical events. As such, they were continuing a trend that has become increasingly significant in the last ten years. If you want your film to be popular, base it on reality. So, to name only a few, we have had in quick succession *The Changeling, the Hurricane, The Aviator, Amelia, Good Night and Good Luck, Edward J, My Week with Marilyn, 127 Hours, The Last of Robin Hood, Behind the Candelabra, and* even two films on the same subject, *Capote* and *Infamous*.

The trend has also hit television, with films on the life of Churchill, on actor Peter Sellers, on writers Ernest Hemingway and Martha Gellhorn, on company scandals, on President Nixon, on the politics of Sarah Palin, on the problems of Wall Street, and on the public and private lives of publishing personalities such as Conrad Black and Robert Maxwell. British TV also ran three films on the life of Prime Minister Margaret Thatcher long before Meryl Streep impersonated her in *The Iron Lady*. Leaving aside biopics, we also have films like *Guyana Tragedy: The Story of Jim Jones*, which would be dismissed as absolutely unbelievable if their stories weren't actually true.

Many of the films are taken from contemporary newspaper headlines, with the newspapers providing a never-ending source of material. For example, a few years ago one item, above all others, dominated the American news media. This was the story of David Koresh and his Branch Davidian cult followers, who were besieged at Waco, Texas, by the FBI. What intrigued me was that Koresh was said to have joked with one reporter as to who would play him in the film. Maybe Tommy Lee Jones or Bruce Willis.

1

The end was no joke. Koresh died in a blazing inferno along with ninety others. Yet he was right. They filmed his story as *Ambush in Waco*, though he didn't stay around long enough to say whether they did a good job.

It was an amazing story. It had sex, charismatic personalities, weirdos, religion, battles, the lot. No writer could have invented a juicier story. Once more, fact was better than fiction.

When thinking about the above phenomena, two things seem clear. Docudramas, or fact-based films, are highly popular in both cinema and on TV. For a jaded audience, they offer something different from the run-of-the-mill comic-book heroes such as Spiderman, Green Lantern, and Batman. They present fascinating characters, with intriguing stories that would be rejected as impossible fictions if one couldn't point to their undeniable base in reality. The second point is that these films are usually highly profitable.

For producers hunting for a killing, there is the knowledge that with the right real-life story, they can really hit the jackpot. Thus *Diana: Her True Story* was seen on almost every television screen throughout the world. Both *The King's Speech* and *The Social Network* proved extremely rewarding financially. And if one were to produce a film about Osama bin Laden's life in Pakistan the year before the Americans hunted him down (which is probably happening as I write), I'm sure the same would be true.

A popular form. An increasing demand. These are intoxicating words for a writer, particularly as writing in this vein is a fairly easy way in for a newcomer. So you say to yourself, "How do I do it? How do I master this genre?" There's the rub. Despite the rise of university and film school courses in scriptwriting, hardly any of these courses deal with the creation of fact-based scenarios. The same is true of film books.

Enter any decent bookstore, and it seems you can find script texts by the dozen, with the most intriguing titles and advice under the sun: how to write a script while in the bath, while repairing your auto, while giving birth; write a script in a week, in a day, in an hour, while having a cup of coffee, while recovering from your operation. All seems fine until you realize the omission. There isn't a single book that attempts to assist in writing the fact-based script.

Could it be that working in this genre presents different challenges compared to in standard genres, and that authors of docudrama are slightly wary of giving advice? Certainly the fact-based film is a complex form that eludes simple rules. It definitely can't be written in five minutes while recovering from a postcoital depression. Whatever the reason, after surveying the field, the would-be writer of docudrama is left with little advice to hand.

The object of this book is to fill that gap: to provide you with a thorough, down-to-earth understanding of all the ins and outs of writing fact-based films, from finding the initial idea to signing off on the finished script.

This is a book about techniques, dramatic conflicts, story agendas, pace, structure, and dialogue writing. It's also a book about television and cinema demands, and ideas that sell. It is also finally a book about ideas and concepts. Its intention is to help you think about the film as a totality, and the nature of the market, before you put a single word on paper.

In essence, this work is about all the problems you face from concept to completion. It deals with ideas—finding them, researching their possibilities in depth, and turning them into viable, gripping stories; it deals with all the stages of script development and fine tuning; it covers experimental forms and hybrid forms; it and touches on the problems of truth and accuracy in your scripts; and it touches on agents, rights, network demands, and legal problems in writing docudrama.

Some topics I explore in depth, and other matters are addressed only briefly. You will see, for example, that the concentration is on writing for features and prime-time television drama, and that other programs that use the factual drama approach, like *Hard Copy*, *NYPD Blue*, *Top Cops*, other true-crime series, and reality TV, hardly get mentioned because of space constraints. I also spend little time on telling you how to sell your screenplay because there are books galore on the subject.

Nor, unfortunately, do I deal with the background and development of docudrama, audience reception, or academic theories and writings on the subject of the fact-fiction film. These topics are fascinating but are for a different book. However, for those of you interested in the broader aspects of the subjects, I would recommend *Docudrama Performs the Past* by Steve Lipkin,[1] *No Other Way to Tell It: Docudrama on Film and Television* by Derek Paget,[2] and my own book *Why Docudrama?*[3]

Instead, the concentration here is on writing: how to develop your skills and realize your potential. In short, the goal is to help you become the terrific writer you always knew you could be.

ORIGINS

This book arose out of a series of course discussions I had with students at the Australian National Film School. The subject was how to go beyond documentary techniques and bring some of its ideas into feature filmmaking. Before we knew it, we were deeply immersed in all the problems and possibilities of writing dramas based on fact.

---

1. Steven Lipkin, *Docudrama Performs the Past* (Newcastle upon Tyne: Cambridge Scholars, 2011).

2. Derek Paget, *No Other Way to Tell It: Docudrama on Film and Television* (Manchester: Manchester University Press, 2011).

3. Alan Rosenthal, *Why Docudrama? Fact-Fiction on Film and TV* (Carbondale: Southern Illinois University Press, 1999).

First, we started exploring the sheer range of fact-based movies and TV dramas, then started hunting for a definition of the subject. Ultimately, these discussions provided the basis for chapters 1 and 2 of this book. One of the most interesting discussions arose out of the question, How would the same subject be treated as a documentary and as a feature? Here we screened three different versions of the story of Aileen Wuornos, who murdered seven men in Florida between 1989 and 1990. The first was a documentary by Nick Broomfield. The second was *Monster*, a feature starring Charlize Theron, while the third was a made-for-TV movie called *Overkill*.

After analyzing the different script approaches used in the Wuornos films, we started looking at some of the other problems of dramadoc, such as creating an interesting script around a dull personality. Here we looked at a few of the letters to Warner Brothers penned by the scriptwriters of *Yankee Doodle Dandy*. The film, which featured James Cagney, tells the story of the rise and success of George M. Cohan, one of America's great songwriters. The problem for the scriptwriters was that Cohan's life was excruciatingly dull, yet the studio contract with Cohan bound the writers to stay close to the truth. So letter after letter from brothers Philip and Julius Epstein, who came in as script doctors, pleads for the right to invent, to create a romance, and to add humor. Finally, the Epstein brothers were allowed a little "creativity," saving what otherwise might have been a very dull picture apart from the songs.

As the course continued, my own interest in dramadoc grew stronger and stronger. I'd written a few pieces in the form, but my own work in the past had mainly been as a writer-director of documentaries. More and more, the writing of fact-based dramas began to appeal to me in a very strong way. I'd always liked the form and, having grown up in England, was very familiar with variations of the form.

Much of the best British cinema output of the Second World War years—for instance, *Target for Tonight*—was expressed in dramadoc form. A few years later, a maverick, Peter Watkins, once more shook the form into life with *Culloden*, a retelling of the last battle between the English and the Scots. Later on, while I was still a film novice, Leslie Woodhead started putting together a specialist dramadoc department at Granada TV. Meanwhile, Peter Goodchild was doing the same thing in London, using BBC Science features as a base for series such as *Marie Curie*.

Gradually, everything started coming together: personal preference, students' needs, and teaching obligations. Before long, I was involved in a mutual exploration with my students regarding the whole question of writing docudrama. All of us were turned on, our heads spinning, as we pondered where we could go with this challenging form.

It was clear to all of us there were a number of absolutely fundamental issues to be resolved. Did normal writing principles apply to this form? How relevant was the standard three-act structure? Did the usual textbook-approved method of hunting for dramatic turning points still work? What liberties could you take with character presentation, and with truth? These were just a few of the questions, but among the most important.

The sessions were challenging, the debates endless, and the working sessions and experiments great. And somewhere along the line, the idea for this book was born.

OBSERVATIONS

This book is laid out in what seems to me the natural progression for thinking and writing about the fact-based script. In the first part, we clear our heads, looking at the popularity of the form and the breadth of the subject, and trying to define the boundaries of docudrama. In the second and third parts, the book addresses the biggest problem at hand: that is, how to write. Here the book discusses ideas, research, proposals, and story definition. It then deals in depth with writing the drama script, and the complications following from the need to adhere to reality and to discuss experimental forms, hybrid forms, These sections represent the core of the book.

Learning to write docudrama is similar to learning to paint. In painting, you can, from the start, if you wish, ignore all rules and paint in the wildest, most experimental way. However, it is probably advisable to get a grounding in the common rules of the craft before proceeding to the wilder shores of creation. Similarly, I think one should understand how basic drama scripts are constructed before getting in the more complex forms of drama.

From the creation of the basic script, the book moves on in the fourth and final part, to some special considerations: adaptations, legends, and rights and legal issues adaptations, and the slippery problem of truth. The final chapter deals with options, legalities, agents, and lawyers, and lastly offers a perspective on the entire process.

This book is designed to help you at whatever stage you're at. You can read it from start to finish, but you don't have to. You may want to skip general discussions and plunge straight into the chapter on finding a subject. Conversely, you may opt to go straight to the chapter on adaptations, as that's the problem that concerns you at the moment. Again, you may want to know more about experimental forms, or your problem may have to do with purchasing an option.

In the end, this is your book, and you have to use it in the way that helps you the most. I hope it will assist you at every stage of the scripting process. Its aim is to make you a competent writer, and also let you know you can have an enjoyable time along the way.

ATTITUDE

Everyone believes he or she can write. Is that true of scripts? Scriptwriting requires resilience, patience, determination, inventiveness, and creativity. Many people have the first three. It's the last two qualities that provide the main stumbling blocks. That's just for starters, without talking about the need for chutzpa (cheek), intelligence, and sometimes even a conscience.

There is also another demand. Beyond understanding the needs of dramatic construction, and how to bring situations and characters—though already based on real people—to life, the writer of docudramas needs a keen sense of journalism. A simple sense of invention is not enough. Very frequently, the story has to be ferreted out, dug up, and wrenched from reams of newspaper reports and court proceedings, and from months of research.

And lurking in all these myriad concerns is the idea of passion. Writing dramadoc is a very interesting way of earning a living. Add passion, belief in your subject, and belief that what you're doing matters, and the whole task takes on a different and possibly more rewarding dimension.

Hotel Rwanda was a script like that, as were *Gandhi, And the Band Played On, United 93, Death of a Princess,* and *Schindler's List.* These were films born out of dreams, born out of fury, anger, involvement. All these scripts, about Gandhi, AIDS, death in a doomed plane, attitudes in Saudi Arabia, and Nazi murderers, reflect a desire to make a statement, to make a movie with meaning, to change the world. Whether they succeeded in this regard or not is almost irrelevant. What remains is their passion, and that was fantastic.

Passion is not always necessary. You can write happily without it, but when you find a film that excites you, that requires passion, only then will you understand what this writing drug is all about.

METHOD

In many ways, books on scriptwriting are like books on dieting. They too offer neatly packaged formulae for success, except they replace inventive menus with shortcut gimmicks and hygienically wrapped rules. Thus the *Scarsdale Diet* turns into *Zarkofski's Guaranteed Script Selling Course,* ten easy rules, and your money returned if you don't sell a script within three months.

Maybe it works, but not for me.

My own method in approaching this book has been relatively simple. I tried to talk to the best professionals around before getting down to work. My questions were always How do you work? and Why do you do things this way?

I asked these professionals about beginnings, structure, and dialogue writing, and also such questions as What do you enjoy most about writing? and What is the most important thing you've learned over the years?

I asked them to tell me about their research problems, to show me their drafts, to let me see their first proposals. This book is a distillation of their advice and represents how experienced professionals tackle the writing of fact-based dramas.

I've included a lot of script extracts, as I believe example and analysis to be very useful teaching tools. Though most of the examples are taken from docudramas, I have occasionally used extracts from fictional films that seemed to illustrate a particular point better than I could find in any fact-based films.

Finally, I have to say that the book also comes out of my own experience as a writer, filmmaker, and teacher and is affected by my quirks, background, experience, and preferences. I have been writing and making films for about twenty-five years and have developed various techniques and approaches that make sense to me. They represent an attempt to put logic into that peculiarly attractive but elusive thing we call scriptwriting.

However, first a warning. All writers are different. The way A approaches a script may differ totally from the way B approaches the same challenge. My method of writing may not work for you. That's fine, so long as you know clearly why your method works best.

What follows from there is that this book isn't sacrosanct. There are no absolute rules in scriptwriting, though there are many hints and suggestions. What is accepted as gospel today may be rejected tomorrow. Monday's three-act structure may get thrown out of the window on Tuesday.

My hope then, is that you'll read this book, accept what is useful, and then turn out a superb script that will show everyone you are for real, and are to be taken seriously as a professional writer.

PART ONE
CLEARING YOUR HEAD

1. THE POPULAR GENRE

Whether you call them docudramas, dramadocs, fact-fiction dramas, or something even more exotic, one thing is clear: reality-based stories are the most popular drama genre on television today. In fact, it would be a most unusual week in which we didn't see at least two or three stories based on real incidents featured on TV. And it's been that way for a long time.

DOCUDRAMA AND TELEVISION

If we were watching a few years ago, the week's films might have centered on victims of appalling crimes. Thus *The Longest Night* told the story of a young woman who was kidnapped and buried alive in a wooden box. But fashions change. A few years later, the fashion was for showing women who had courageously overcome illnesses and physical handicaps to take up or resume careers, as actresses or sportswomen. So we were treated to the stories of Patricia Neal, on CBS; and Maureen Connolly, Little Mo, on NBC.

However, the public is fickle. Tastes change. Tomorrow, murder may be out and the private lives of politicians even more popular. In fact, the trend has already begun, with TV and feature films on Franklin D. Roosevelt, Winston Churchill, Margaret Thatcher, Ronald Reagan, Richard Nixon, Bill Clinton, Hilary Clinton, and Sarah Palin jostling each other for air time. In some senses, it's all a guessing game. Yet underneath all this, and regardless of changing fashions and subjects, two highly provocative and encouraging facts stare the writer in the face.

First, the public loves docudrama, or dramadocs, which for the sake of simplicity are the terms I'm going to use most throughout this book. Second, there is a bustling, thriving market out there for good scripts. Never has there been a better time than now for the writer to plunge in and master the genre. Consistently through the 1990s and first decade of this century, about 30 percent of made-for-TV movies were docudramas. And of these made-for-TV movies, usually about six out of the top ten highest-rated movies were based on real-life happenings.

Popularity and high ratings: these are the goals producers dream about, and for which network executives are practically willing to kill. No wonder the pursuit of the best-selling docudrama formula has a very high priority. Sometimes, the hunt reaches the height of the absurd when we see different networks and cable stations issuing films on the same subject within weeks, if not days, of each other. The ultimate absurdity took place in 1993 when all three major networks featured dramas about a would-be teenage killer called Amy Fisher. And in our own time, two films about Truman Capote, *Capote* and *Infamous* came out within nine months of each other. The same was true for Alfred Hitchcock when two films about him, *Hitchcock* and *The Girl*, were both released in 2012.

This race for the best-selling formula doesn't embrace just aging music stars, nubile murderesses, actors, sportsmen and -women, and Marilyn Monroe and the Kennedy clan. It hunts around the world's disasters, politics, and gossip columns and even has the audacity to pry into palace bedrooms. Thus, before Princess Diana's death, there were four major TV films made in the U.S. dealing with the stormy relations between Prince Charles and Diana. And since her death, we have seen *The Murder of Princess of Diana*, and *Hidden Truth*. More recently we have had *William and Kate*, dealing with the romance of the presumed current heir to the throne.

In any discussion, however brief, one thing emerges very clearly. The U.S. networks, in general, tend to stay away from all but the most sensational hard news and political stories and tend to go for more personal biopics and human conflicts. Films about the Waco tragedy or the Twin Towers bombing are the exception, not the rule. This simple home truth has to be borne in mind when you start considering where to devote your efforts.

Yet the dramatic journalistic news story has, in its own small way, found an honored niche in docudrama, with British television in the vanguard. On the American side, HBO is the only company that can be considered deeply involved in this more serious fare.

I deliberately said "honored niche" because it seems to me that the political dramadoc is in many ways much more fascinating, more challenging, and ultimately more rewarding for a writer than the standard movie of the week. It is certainly fascinating to write, though as you'll see, it tends to present many more problems than the standard biopic. I also believe it is more highly regarded by the public, though this doesn't necessarily translate into higher ratings.

What are some good examples of this genre? I would definitely cite in any list of favorites *The Tragedy of Flight 103*, about the downing of a Pan Am plane over Scotland by Arab terrorists; *Skokie*, about a neo-Nazi march through a suburb of Chicago; *Who Bombed Birmingham?*, about the blowing up of a pub in Birmingham, England; and *Death of a Princess*, about the execution of a Saudi Arabian princess and her lover in an Arabian marketplace.

DOCUDRAMA AND THE FEATURE FILM

If television is a great marketplace for docudrama, what about the docudrama feature film marketplace? Are there the same possibilities? Are there the same opportunities for writers? What about the scope, the current situation, and the future? Now, I'm lousy at predicting the future, but it seems to me the reality of the situation is as follows.

Marketplace

Fewer features are made than TV films, and of those made, a much smaller percentage is devoted to stories based on real happenings. However, the situation seems to be in flux, with the public drawn more and more to reality-based films. According to the yearbook of Britain's Film Distributors' Association docudramas made up about 10 percent of the top one hundred films screened in England in 2003. Between 2005 and 2006, biopics alone included films about Ray Charles, Alfred Kinsey, and Howard Hughes (*Ray*, *Kinsey*, *The Aviator*).

Events from recent history have also continued to inspire the feature docudrama. Thus, in 2005, ten years after the genocidal horrors in Rwanda, we saw *Hotel Rwanda*, followed by *Shooting Dogs* and *100 Days*. A year later, the first attack on the Twin Towers was featured in Oliver Stone's *World Trade Center*. In 2011 and 2012, five out of the ten Oscar candidates for best picture were docudramas, with *The King's Speech* winning in 2011. In 2013, three of the Oscar candidates for best film, *Argo*, *Lincoln*, and *Zero Dark Thirty*, were docudramas, with *Argo* winning the prize. Furthermore, directors like Clint Eastwood seem to be drawn to the genre, with Eastwood himself being responsible for three recent reality films, including *The Changeling*, *Letters from Iwo Jima*, and *Flags of Our Fathers*.

Scope

There is another aspect to the story. Though in numbers the feature marketplace is smaller than the TV marketplace, the scope and rewards, including public recognition, are greater for the writer in this area than on TV. What is also very attractive for a writer is that he or she can work with a much larger budget and on a much bigger canvas, and can aim to tell stories that would be virtually impossible to tell on TV.

David Lean's *Lawrence of Arabia*, with a script by Robert Bolt, works fantastically on film. The wide screen adds a breathtaking sweep to the astounding views of the Jordanian desert that make for half the film's attraction. A similar magic is to be found in the panoramic vision of India in Richard Attenborough's *Gandhi*. However, it would be hard to imagine either of them being made as television originals.

The same is true for *Mutiny on the Bounty*. Like Lean's desert epic, *Mutiny* allowed for wide-scale action, panorama, pounding seas, landscapes, and photographic vision, all more suitable for film than television.

Historical romances and adventures have of course been a steady source of inspiration for Hollywood, particularly in the area of the western and the gangster movie. The Jesse James gang is forever riding into the sunset. Billy the Kid is being shot down for the fifteenth time by Pat Garrett. Al Capone is snarling, and Legs Diamond romancing another moll. All good clean or dirty fun, but not much of it based on fact. However, the 2009 film *Public Enemies*, about John Dillinger, shows that this may be changing, but I'm not sure. The irony of these kinds of films is that the writers spend months researching but don't come up with much that resembles reality or has anything to do with this book. When fiction and invention account for so large a portion of the script, we are into standard scriptwriting, and that's something for another time and another place.

So to return to the recent Oscar nominees of 2011, 2012, and 2013, what does it all mean? Apart from teenagers, is the audience growing tired of comic-book fantasies, does it want its films to grow out of authentic, documented, real-life situations? Given the success of *Hugo, Warhorse, Avatar*, and *The Adventures of Tintin*, I doubt that, but I do think change is in the air.

So, with no real claims to prophesy, I would say one thing is clear. If you have a good real-life story to relate, and can write a good screenplay from such a story, then the market in the coming decade is probably the best and most receptive it's been in years.

2. WHAT IS DOCUDRAMA?

You want to write reality-based dramas, and fact-fiction, but wait a minute. What are we talking about? What is this strange form that floats somewhere between documentary and fiction. What is docudrama?

As a kid growing up in England, I would occasionally visit the British Museum. One stone carving at the entrance fascinated me above all others. This was a huge sculpture of an amazing animal. The body was that of a bull. Its head was that of a bearded man. It had wings, and the tail of a lion. Altogether it was a very strange beast. Only later did I realize I was looking at an apt concrete metaphor for the fact-based drama, which too, is a most peculiar animal.

First, there is the difficulty of the name, and the bewildering labeling. *Docudrama. Dramadoc. Dramatic reconstruction. Murdofact. Reality-based film. Fact-based drama. Biopic.*

Where will it all end? Maybe we should announce a competition for something definitive, but that might bring worse horrors: "factovies" or "factoramas." For simplicity's sake, and as there is no one accepted name for the genre, I am mostly going to us the terms *docudrama* or *dramadocs* throughout this book.

Of course, the real problem is defining what we are talking about. A prosaic but useful and workman-like definition of TV docudrama is that given by Tom Hoffer and Richard Alan Nelson, two American academics. They call it:

> A unique blend of fact and fiction which dramatizes events and historic personages from our recent memory.... It is a TV recreation based on fact even though it relies on actors, dialogue, sets, and costumes to recreate an earlier event. The accuracy and comprehensiveness of such a recreation . . . can vary widely and is conditioned not only by intent but also by factors such as budget and production time.[1]

Leslie Woodhead, a very distinguished maker of English docudramas, puts the problem a little differently:

1. Tom Hoffer and Richard Alan Nelson, "Docudrama on American Television," *Journal of the UFA* 30 (Spring 1978): 21.

We filmmakers swap labels like baseball cards. One of my colleagues has identified three major strands to the form while another has isolated six varieties. . . . At the end of last year I found myself on a platform for yet another drama-doc tussle with no fewer than seven distinguished program makers who used the form. You won't be surprised to hear that no two of us could agree on what it is.

However, after describing the confusion, Woodhead presented a handy way of looking at the problem.

[Instead of hunting for definitions] I think it much more useful to think of the form as a spectrum that runs from journalistic reconstructions to relevant drama with infinite graduations along the way. In its various mutations it's employed by investigative journalists, documentary feature makers, and imaginative dramatists.[2]

Woodhead's presentation is excellent, though many would dispute the word *relevant*. Are all the dramas about the royal family and Diana relevant? Not really. And can this word be applied to the hullabaloo about the teenage shooter Amy Fisher? Or *My Week with Marilyn*? Probably not, but were these programs fun and amusing? Yes, I think so.

The real operative word is *spectrum*. If you wanted, you could claim that fact-based drama goes back to Shakespeare. In other words, docudrama covers an amazing variety of dramatic forms, bound together by two things. First, they are all *based on* or *inspired by* reality, by the lives of real people, or events that have happened in the recent or not too distant past. Second, for this reason, they have a higher responsibility for accuracy and truth than fiction does.

But, again, there are limitations. Many of the scripts in the popular TV series *The Defenders* were inspired by current news stories. However, they did not purport to present real events or real people and were totally fictitious. To my mind, they were not docudramas, and I spend little time on that kind of script in these pages. Similarly, the films of Tony Parker are not docudramas. Tony, an English scriptwriter, did immense amounts of research in English prisons and used the material to write some very successful and moving TV plays, which were presented in a very realistic style. These fictions I would call documentary-style dramas, not docudramas.

For the writer, the sheer breadth of the spectrum makes reality-based dramas both highly attractive, and also immensely problematic. In a form that runs the gamut from biopics like *Yankee Doodle Dandy* and *The Iron Lady* to political analyses such as *JFK*, it sometimes happens that you can't see the forest for the trees. For myself, I see docudrama as a form divided into two main strands or two separate areas.

2. Leslie Woodhead, "The Guardian Lecture," London, 1980.

BIOGRAPHY AND ENTERTAINMENT

This category probably makes up 90 percent of the docudramas we see in the cinema and on TV. It runs from *Sergeant York* to *Capote, J. Edgar,* and *My Week with Marilyn.* It includes *Bird, Public Enemies, The Life and Death of Peter Sellers,* and miniseries about Frank Sinatra and about the Kennedy and Jackson families. It also includes all the current titillating murders of the week.

What generally categorizes these films and scripts are a desire for the highest audience ratings, an emphasis on entertainment values, and a rather loose regard for truth and accuracy. When they are made for U.S. television networks, they tend to come under the supervision of the drama departments rather than news and documentary.

RECONSTRUCTIVE INVESTIGATIONS

Though highly honored, this is a much smaller category and includes pieces such as *Death of a Princess; United 93; Hostages; JFK; Dr. Death; And the Band Played On; The Tragedy of Flight 103; Who Bombed Birmingham?;* and *Dead Ahead: The Exxon Valdez Disaster* (presented by the BBC as *Exxon Valdez*).

What we are looking at here is a very serious form, much closer to journalism and news than to conventional drama. Though it uses dramatic forms, characters, sets, and written dialogue, its motivating force is the restless inquirer and the investigative reporter. It wants to uncover and reveal for the public good, and not just in the name of higher ratings. Its highest goal is to present a powerful enthralling drama that nevertheless gets as close to the truth as possible. This is what gives the genre its moral imperative, and separates it, when it is at its best, so clearly from the usual fictional drama.

Leslie Woodhead, who has done some of the best films in this category, such as *Invasion,* about the 1968 Russian invasion of Czechoslovakia, calls it the form of last resort. "It's a way of doing things where ordinary documentary can't cope . . . a way of telling a story that would be impossible by conventional documentary methods."

Obviously, there is a tremendous overlap in the categories. Some while ago, HBO made a three-hour film about Stalin, with Robert Duvall. The reviews varied. Some critics were put off by the emphasis on Stalin's private life. Personally I felt that the domestic scenes were necessary to reveal the inner man and acted as an interesting counterpoint to the overtly political portions of the film. What one got in the end was a fascinating combination of news and private-life drama.

Does it matter? So what if edges blur! Does one always have to think in categories? Maybe not, but I still think there is a case for making lists. Such actions help you define where you want to go as a writer, and what your task is on a particular subject. Thinking briefly about your choices— journalism, entertainment bios, or anything else—helps you to clarify your approach.

Writing dramadocs is not easy. The form is seductive, entrancing, fascinating, but also very complex. To my mind, it's much more appealing than writing comic-book action adventures, but you have to watch out. There are many traps along the way. So the clearer you are as to where you want to go, what your objectives are, and how you want to get there, the easier the whole task becomes.

3. CHOOSING A DYNAMIC SUBJECT

On Sunday, November 22, 1992, the front page of the arts and leisure section of the *New York Times* bore the legend "MURDER, MAYHEM STALK TV. Television in frenzy over real-life sagas." Although the article discussed TV docudrama in general, its main story dealt with the strange and lurid case of Amy Fisher.

This seventeen-year-old young lady had fallen in love with a garage mechanic called Joey Buttafuoco. The fact that Joey was married was seen by Amy as only a minor hindrance to true love. So armed with a loaded pistol, she had taken a pop at Joey's wife, Mary Jo, wounding her but not killing her. For this act, Amy was later sentenced to five to fifteen years imprisonment.

This time, not one, not two, but all three major networks saw in this story the seeds of a best-selling docudrama. They were right; NBC's film got one of the highest film ratings of the season.

The most interesting aspect of the whole affair is not the Fisher story itself—rather a dull, tawdry tale as tales go—but the rush for the rights. Was it a great story? No! Was it an unusual story? No! Yet all three networks were correct in sensing that this story would whet the jaded palates of millions of Americans needing rest and titillation after a hard day's work. As John O'Connor wrote later in the *New York Times*, "No network has yet gone broke overestimating its audience's appetite for sleaze."

Here, three producers guessed correctly that the story would appeal to a mass audience on TV. But often it is the writer who has the idea and takes it to the producer. So for the writer to be worth anything, he or she has to be able to pick out the story, the situation, or idea that can be the basis for a successful screenplay.

The first questions then appear to be:
Where can I find and choose ideas?
Does the story have audience appeal?
Can I sell it to a producer?
Does the subject really attract me as a writer?

The questions of appeal and marketability are the background constants always in your mind, and against which any subject is tested. However, as this book is about writing rather than selling, I've left my comments on the marketplace to appendix B. Appeal is a different matter entirely and is worth considering before we even begin thinking about specific ideas.

THE APPEAL

A writer needs to understand his or her audience. He or she needs to understand the audience's demands, what satisfies them, what they want to look at, and what works and doesn't work for them. He or she needs to know what makes for irresistible viewing, and what turns the audience off.

In short, you need to know . . . what appeals to the masses.

Of course, if you knew that answer, and were right even 70 percent of the time, you'd be a millionaire. Clearly, we are talking of the almost impossible ideal. Yet we have to understand the concept, because if your story has no appeal, it's doomed. You need to consider the elements of appeal before you even begin to consider writing a story. Your stories will change, but your understanding of what might or might not make them work for an audience is your initial guide of whether or not to proceed with your endeavor.

TRUTH IS STRANGER THAN FICTION

In terms of appeal, you have, of course, a terrific initial advantage without doing anything. The very act of choosing to write a reality-based drama already puts you ahead of the game.

Why should that be?

It seems to me almost axiomatic to say that when you have two similar stories— one true, one invented—the former has greater appeal. The sense that this strange event actually happened holds a psychological fascination for us that is missing in invention. The story is closer to us and often affects us in strange and deep ways that are usually inaccessible to fiction.

In 1993, Disney Studios made *Alive*, based on the true story of a Uruguayan rugby team whose plane had crashed in the Andes in 1972. Sixteen members of the team, many under the age of twenty, survived over two months in the mountains by eating those who had died. The book on the incident had been a best seller but had bounced around various studios for years until Disney finally picked it up.

Resorting to cannibalism for survival is an extremely strong theme, and not new to literature or history. Thus the story of the survival of some of the Donner party lost in the winter in the Rockies is one of the most heart-rending events in U.S. history. But both the story of the Donner party and the epic of the rugby team get their strength from being true. Imagine both stories as fiction, and you can see immediately what is lost.

The movie *127 Hours* tells the true story of a mountain climber trapped under a boulder, who cut off his arm in order to survive. Similarly, *Touching the Void* tells the miraculous story of a man who survived death when he plunged down a mountain in Peru. If the stories had been fiction, we would probably have said "forget it." Instead, we rushed to see the films.

A similar brush-off might have occurred had *Schindler's List* and *In the Name of the Father* not been based on reality. The story of how Oskar Schindler saved nearly a thousand Jews from the Nazi death camps is one of the most bizarre stories to come out of the Second World War. As fiction, it would have been forgettable melodrama. As truth, it takes its place as one of the most emotional and moving films ever made.

For its part, *In the Name of the Father* presents us with a classic miscarriage-of-justice story, not exactly a new theme in the annals of the cinema. Here, again, reality, plus the power of the directing, lifts a film from banality to create a tremendously memorable film experience.

The Dramatic Elements

For your story to appeal, it has to have drama, conflict, strong characters caught up interesting situations, and a satisfying resolution.

Well, that was an easy one!

Not really, because the elements mentioned above are going to be discussed over and over again in this book. The point here is that you have to recognize when you have hit on the right context which enables you to play around with all the above elements. Not all conflicts between characters or situations are worth our attention. The *L.A. Times* doesn't pay much attention to what's happening in Botswana because it knows its readers couldn't care less. In contrast, it pays a lot of attention to what's happening in Russia, and even more to signs of clashes in the White House.

Again, not all characters are worth a glance. Write a drama about John Major, a former English prime minister, and his governmental problems, and the audience will be asleep in two minutes. Give them a bloodthirsty tyrant like Stalin, or a stuttering shy English king, and they'll come back clamoring for more.

Elements That Inspire Passion

What we need to train ourselves to do is to look at the forces underlying the conflicts, whether political or human: the passion, the fury, the emotional hunger, and the need for sex or for fame at all cost. In other words, we have to look at the emotional turn-ons that fascinate us. The devils that drove Charlie Parker and Sylvia Plath; the intense ambition that sparked Bill Gates and Steve Jobs; the attractions and feuds of Ernest Hemingway and war reporter Martha Gellhorn.

No one knows this better than the *National Enquirer*, one of the best-selling papers in the U.S. Every time I go to the supermarket, I am amazed by its headline. A typical story might read as follows:

> Flash. Elvis Presley is alive on Mars. He has had a sex change, practices Buddhism, and says he killed Marilyn Monroe at the bidding of President Kennedy.

Of course, no one would believe it, but that's not the issue. It's a stupid story, but people would love it, because it encompasses so many of the elements our psyches openly or secretly crave or are passionately interested in:

Sex
Sensation
Action
Violence
The inside dope on the great and famous
A normal world turned upside down
Fanaticism

Analyze any top-rated TV movie of the week, and you'll probably find it contains at least four or five of the above elements. There's a lesson here. Whereas a moralist might agonize over the debased delights of the average viewer, the writer notes what interests the TV audience and acts accordingly.

In 1991, a Mormon father of eight killed a nurse and a doctor. He believed a child was waiting in heaven to be born to him and that the doctor had sterilized his wife against her will. Describing this incident, a journalist wrote, "This tale has all the elements of a TV hit: birth, death, religion, terror, insanity, remorse."

This illustrates that what often seems to appeal are pictures about human actions pushed to the edge, behavior that runs against all our norms, behavior that we cannot understand but which nevertheless fascinates us.

On the positive side, this behavior is captured in the mad, heroic drive of Captain Scott heading for the South Pole, or Burke and Wills exploring nineteenth-century Australia. On the negative side, there are the stories of Koresh and his band, and the grim story of the footballers who turned to cannibalism in *Alive*.

The Psychological Appeal

The appeal of the docudrama is not limited solely to the public's voyeuristic interests relating to sex, crime, and violence. I think docudrama also helps to satisfy the public's appetite for information, while also providing it with an opportunity to debate historical, social, and political issues.

While discussing trends on television in *DGA Quarterly*, the journal of the Directors Guild of America, producer Tony Eltz put the matter this way: "There's a value for the viewer in seeing that a very scary thing has an explanation. For example we recently produced *Deadly Medicine*, which helped viewers to understand why a nurse might be driven to murder 32 babies."

John Matoian, a former CBS vice president, has his own comments on the appeal of the murder dramadocs. "People are looking for windows into behavior. Hopefully they'll gain insight from these kinds of movies."

Maybe, but I doubt it. My feeling is that raw voyeurism comes first in appeal and all social explanations are secondary.

The Appeal of the Genre

Another way of looking at appeal is to leave out psychological speculation, and merely look at the genres that seem to have had a continuing attraction over time. Obviously, the genres intertwine, and many times subjects can be seen to straddle different categories. A simplified rundown of groupings would clearly include the following.

Secrets behind closed doors. This area includes exposés of the rich and the famous. It touches on their dark, hidden lives and quite often reveals sexual scandals. Examples would include *Scandal, Diana: Her True Story,* and *J.F.K: Reckless Youth.*

The lives of entertainers and artists. This group is staple fare for both TV and film. It includes *Bird*, about the troubled life and career of jazz musician Charlie Parker; *Van Gogh*, about the last days of the artist; *Liz and Dick*, about the roller coaster relationship between Richard Burton and Elizabeth Taylor; *Pollock*, about the career of Jackson Pollock; and *The Life and Death of Peter Sellers*. So, with luck, not only do we see the entertainers act, dance, sing, and paint, we also often get a story replete with sex and drugs. So everyone is satisfied.

Sometimes, the net goes wider. What was interesting in 2012 was to see two very different films devoted to the career and work of Alfred Hitchcock. So the telefilm *The Girl* showed Hitchcock's sexual infatuation with Tippi Hedren, star of *The Birds*. By way of contrast, the feature film *Hitchcock* dealt with the relations between the director and his wife, and the making of *Psycho*.

The private and public lives of heroes. Here, the attempt is made to understand the movers of history, to get behind the public mask, and to understand the real, private person. Examples include *The Queen*, and *The Iron Lady* and range from films on Gandhi, Churchill, and Stalin, to examinations of the careers of Kinsey, Freud, and even L. Ron Hubbard, the founder of Scientology.

If the film's main characters are true adventurers, then even better. This accounts for the success of films like *Amelia* and *The Spirit of St. Louis*, about early aviation heroes, or *Shackleton*, about Ernest Shackleton's 1914 "Endurance" expedition to the South Pole.

Understanding history. This group often overlaps the previous one, but the emphasis is on the events and the historic process, rather than on the individual. Here, I would again cite *Stalin*, and include *And the Band Played On*, about AIDS, and *Thirteen Days*, about the Cuban missile crisis.

Investigating contemporary events. The aim in this category, which is huge, is to make a dramatic and penetrating analysis of national or world events that have captured the public imagination. The stories behind the Beirut hostages, the attack on bin Laden's fortress, and the plane attack on the World Trade Center and its aftermath are good examples. A growing trend has been to cover interesting economic stories or phenomena in such films as *The Barbarians at the Gate*, *The Social Network*, and *Pirates of Silicon Valley*, about the phenomenal rise of Bill Gates and Steve Jobs.

Crime and lurid scandals. This area provides the hottest hunting ground for TV. The genre covers all the small-town, titillating crimes of sex and violence and aberrant human behavior that provide the staple diet of *People* magazine. This is *Peyton Place*, but for real.

These are stories that acquaint us with such alleged murderesses or would-be murderesses as Amy Fisher, Wanda Holloway in *Willing to Kill*, and Carolyn Warmus. Serial killers are also in. So, in 2012, the ITV mini-series *Appropriate Adult*, about Fred West, who tortured, raped and murdered fifteen women in England, not only was extremely popular but also collected two prestigious BAFTAs (British Academy of Film and Television Arts awards), Britain's highest TV award.

Weird human behavior. This is really a subcategory of contemporary events and lurid scandals (one is tempted to say "Thank God, enough is enough") and includes the exploits of David Koresh and Jim Jones. But as I believe the public appetite is growing for the bizarre, I have a horrible feeling this genre is ready to become a growth industry.

Stories of love and that touch the heart. Certain stories have a way of touching the soul, of bonding people. These are often stories of community endeavor, of family sacrifice, of battling against illness, and so on. And if they contain kids or animals, even better.

When an eighteen-month-old baby fell into and was trapped in a well in Texas, she became an instant celebrity. When she was saved, *Everybody's Baby: The Rescue of Jessica McClure* became one of the most widely viewed films on TV.

Sylvia and *Iris* are slightly different. Whereas *Sylvia* told of the love and battles between the poets Sylvia Plath and Ted Hughes, and Sylvia's eventual suicide, *Iris* dealt with the love and devotion of novelist Iris Murdoch's husband, John Bailey, after Iris became stricken with Alzheimer's disease.

FINDING A STORY

You know all about appeal. Now all you have to do is go out and find a good story. At this point, it's not uncommon to feel like the guy who has read all the right books on sex and romance but still balks at the hunt and the chase. Courage is the answer. Now is the time to abandon theory and get down to action. And it's not that hard.

The stories are all around you—in books and articles, on television, on the web, and on the radio. They arise from anecdotes of friends, from a story in a diary, from the memory of a relative.

Your sources are fairly obvious.

Books: *Goodfellas, Papillon, Public Enemies, The Accidental Billionaires, Diana: Her True Story, The Fighter*
Newspapers and magazine articles: *The Killing Fields, Fatal Memories, Andy and Fergie, Dr. Death, Who Bombed Birmingham?*
Radio and TV: *Skokie, Flight 93*, and the films on Koresh and the Twin Towers
Plays: *Frost/Nixon*

Obviously, a great number of sources overlap. What appears in the newspapers will also be on TV. But not always.

What you should be looking for is either the "hot" story or the unknown. The first is very appealing, but very difficult to bring off. Today, most networks and major producers of docudramas not only employ scouts to search for hot stories but also spend vast amounts of money purchasing the story rights, if necessary.

In this context, the most dramatic illustration was the media pursuit of the Nancy Kerrigan and Tonya Harding story. Everyone understood very quickly that nothing could be more Hollywood than the story of a beautiful ice-skater whose Olympic dreams were nearly shattered by the henchmen of her fiercest rival. The story had greed, a beautiful heroine, and proper villains. Over forty companies vied for the rights, with producer Steve Tisch finally making an alleged million-dollar deal with Kerrigan.

A few years ago, a local newspaper might pick up on a small-town scandal that would then come to the eye of a writer. Today, that all seems ancient history. In its place are specialized services such as L.A.-based Industry R&D (IRD), which was established to search for sensational tabloid news.

The situation does not seem to leave much room or leverage for the average writer. That's not to say it's impossible to find the dynamic story before anyone else—in fact, the authors of *Silkwood* did just that—just that usually it's very difficult getting control of all the elements. But a factor in your favor is that a story may exist that everyone has missed. Thus the facts behind *The*

King's Speech had been known for years before writer David Seidler wrote the subject into a script that would make a good film.

Chariots of Fire presents a similar example. While searching through a bookcase, producer David Puttnam came across the history of the 1924 Olympic games, where two British runners won gold under very interesting conditions. David's friends doubted there was a story there but were around to clap when the film won an Oscar.

It's also worth considering the origins of *Death of a Princess*, one of the most famous British docudramas ever made. In 1978, an item appeared in most Western newspapers, along the lines of "Saudi Arabian princess shot to death while her lover is beheaded." For a few days, the item grabbed the headlines but was then quickly forgotten. Except by one man: Antony Thomas.

Thomas, a noted British documentary filmmaker, had become intrigued by everything that *wasn't* mentioned in the news. Who was the princess? Why was she killed? Under what circumstances?

Thomas got ATV to back his research, which took him through the Middle East. The resulting film, *Death of a Princess*, was widely shown in Europe and the U.S. and is generally regarded as one of the classics of docudrama. This ability, like Thomas's, to ferret out a story, or see possibilities that no one else has thought of, is absolutely essential for a writer.

Looking for the Winner

When I was putting this chapter together, I thought I'd set myself an exercise. I thought I'd start looking for ideas, the same as you. I would file them away, tell you later where I found them, and try to justify my interest in them.

The elements I would look for would include everything we've discussed so far. Stories with conflict, passion, sex, jealousy, murder. The only things I demanded from all of them was that they should have clear "heroes" and strong dramatic potential. Here are a few of them.

The case of Judge Wachtler. I saw this story in the *New York Times*. Sol Wachtler was a former New York state chief justice who had hopes of being governor. After investigation, he was sentenced to fifteen months in prison for threatening to kidnap the daughter of his former lover, Joy Silverman.

Among other things, the story involved the sending of obscene letters, and the hiring by Wachtler of a private eye to stalk his lover, and threatening her with compromising photographs of her with her new lover.

The story had unbelievable actions by a senior judge. It had cops and sex. It had the mighty brought low. It was a sad human story, but great for TV. The same was true of the film *Strange Justice*, which recreated the confrontation between Clarence Thomas and Anita Hill over sexual misconduct during his Supreme Court confirmation hearings.

The story of Dominique Strauss-Kahn. Again, this is a story of how the mighty are fallen. Strauss-Kahn was a prominent French economist and also a member of the French parliament. He was at one time managing director of the International Money Fund, and a possible French presidential candidate. However, in 2011, he was accused of having sexually assaulted a maid in the Sofitel hotel in New York. He was arrested, held in custody for a while, then released when his accuser's credibility was questioned. Subsequently, rumors arose of possible similar incidents in France, which he denied. Again, fruitful pickings for a docudrama with international appeal.

The Costa Concordia *disaster.* As every producer knows, there's nothing like a good disaster to boost ratings. On January 13, 2012 the Italian ship *Costa Concordia* ran aground on a reef very close to the Italian coast. Twenty-five people died. But it was not an act of God. Immediately, blame was placed on the captain, who was said to be showing off to onlookers back on shore. He was said to be without glasses. To be dallying with a young lady at the time of the disaster. To have leaped into a life boat immediately, with no thought of the passengers. Yet some journalists claimed too hasty a rush to judgment. Though not quite shades of the *Titanic* story, I certainly thought there was material there for a dramadoc.

The code breakers. This time it was a headline in the London *Times* that caught my eye. "Codebreakers reunion sheds light on Enigma." The article itself was about a reunion in London of wartime code breakers.

In the Second World War, they had all lived together in a house in London. Many were mathematicians. Others were chess players and crossword solvers. They looked like a group of out-of-work university professors. Appearances were deceptive. Among them, they cracked the vital German, Italian, and Japanese secret codes to reveal the enemies' movements, plans, and strategy.

Here, I thought the story had possibilities in all directions. We had crazy personalities who in their own secret way were doing as much to win the war as Patton or Montgomery. They were "the quiet heroes" and definitely story material.

The terrorist. In summer 2011 a young man, Anders Behring Brevik, murdered sixty-seven people, mostly under the age of thirty, on the island of Utoya, Norway. This was after he had already blown up a government building in Oslo. The murders hit world headlines. At his trial, Brevik was unrepentant, claiming that what he did was for the good of Norway. Here, the story could go various ways. One could explore the background and nature of Brevik. The film might be an excuse to look at immigration and right-wing movements in Norway. Or it could look at the actions of the police, who arrived so late at the scene.

PROPOSALS AND PITCHING

In the opening of Robert Altman's film *The Player*, we see two writers feverishly trying to persuade a jaded Hollywood producer to back a script. To make their point, they act out their story in forty seconds, trying to give it pathos, humor, drama, and tragedy.

This is what we call *the pitch*. You may be involved in this experience, in which case, God help you; but more likely you will have first done a proposal.

A proposal is a short description of the film you want to do, and its objective is to fire the interest of a producer to back the project. It's a prospectus, a sales document, a device to sell a film idea. It's not nearly as elaborate or worked out as a treatment (which we'll discuss later) but should show clearly what the film is about and where it's going.

Generally, the proposal is used by the independent writer when the story is a little off the beaten track, and he or she has to persuade a producer or a TV commissioning editor that the story is interesting, and potentially has strong audience appeal. Where the story is well known, such as the *Costa Concordia* sinking, or the Chilean mine disaster of 2010, the writer would probably just pitch the idea and not bother with a formal proposal. However, many networks and producers still like to see a formal proposal so that any oral discussions can be more concrete.

There is no standard form for a proposal. Try to keep it short rather than long, as few producers have much patience to read anything of great length. In any case, all you are trying to do is inspire initial interest. The real work comes later.

In your proposal, you set out the most attractive aspects of your idea. You explain its drawing power, its topicality, its relevance, and its potential audience. If it's for television, you may want to suggest a particular slot for your idea such as *History Mysteries* or *FBI True Stories*. All these things help your proposal, but in the end only one thing matters: is your story any good? You therefore usually set out a short synopsis of the story, making it as colorful, dramatic, and powerful as you can.

Below, by way of example, I've set out the short version of a proposal I wrote some years ago, which was eventually taken up by ZDF, Germany.

THE FIRST FAGIN
Proposal for a Ninety-Minute Documentary Drama Feature

A TV special for the Dickens bicentennial in 2012 about the man who inspired the creation of Fagin.

In May 1827 a man was about to stand trial in Britain, accused of theft and receiving stolen goods. If found guilty he would either hang or be transported to Australia. However a day before trial, he made a

sensational escape from London's notorious Newgate prison and fled
to America. More incredible news followed. The man found that a few
weeks after his disappearance, his beloved wife Ann had been framed
by the police in revenge for his flight. Together with her children she
had been sent as a convict to the penal colony of Van Diemen's Land
(today Tasmania). In an act of folly, based on mad devotion and passion, the man (still wanted by the British police) then sailed to the notorious penal colony to rejoin his wife and family and ease their plight.

For months the newspapers talked of little else. For here was no
ordinary fugitive from justice. The man on the run was the great Ikey
Solomon, the most famous criminal of his time. A man who like Fed-
erer, Michael Jackson or Osama Bin Laden today, totally captured the
imagination of the general public.

**Later, when the author Charles Dickens created his most famous
character Fagin, in "Oliver Twist," it is our belief that he was almost
totally inspired by the model of Ikey Solomon . . . an intriguing idea,
which our film examines in depth.**

In "The First Fagin" we bring to life the dramatic turbulent career
of Ikey Solomon, one of Australia and England's most famous convicts
and icons. As we follow Ikey's journey we also observe the grim system
of British justice and transportation which took Ikey from his life as
a prosperous ruffian in London's east end to exile in a penal colony at
the end of the earth. The film is also the story of blind love and devotion as Ikey crosses half the world to save his wife in Hobart. Here he
lives with her as a freeman but is recognized, reported, captured, and
shipped to Britain in chains, to take center stage in London's most famous trial of the day—a trial that now returns him as a convict to Van
Diemen's where love had borne him only a few years before.

Using Ikey's amazing tale as the backbone of our story, the main
thrust of the film is to examine the meaning of crime and punishment
in 19th century England and Australia. Thus following Ikey's career we
move from the thieves dens, criminal courts, sordid jails and public ex-
ecutions in London to the rocky coasts of Australia and Van Diemen's
land. On the way we observe the workings of the grim convict transportation system, that brought over 100,000 convicts to the area. Once
in Van Diemen's Land we look at the daily life of the exiled convicts,
the chain gangs around Hobart, and the brutality of the prisons in
Richmond and Port Arthur.

Method of Filming

The film will be done as a documentary and drama reconstruction feature. It is related by Ikey himself from his prison cell in Van
Diemen's Land. There he recalls his life as the most successful fence,

or receiver of stolen goods, in the crime ridden London of the time. We see him as child pick pocket, and youthful criminal sentenced to seven years on the Hulks, the floating prisons that dotted the Thames, and his amazing rise to be the most successful criminal of his time,—a man who commanded respect, celebrity, and even affection among the teeming poor of London's East End, for whom he was a kind of hero. He then recalls his downfall, his life on the run, the ruin of his wife, and the madness that took him to Australia and the penal colony.

As Ikey's story unfolds, Dickens also strides across the scene, observing, and noting reality while his fiery imagination gradually creates the character of Fagin.

The filmic method is to mix reenacted scenes with straight documentary location shooting. Very often the reenacted scenes, such as life in Newgate prison, or at a hanging, will be covered by Ikey's observations. There will be a minimum of actors' dialogue in these scenes. Other scenes such as Hobart jail, or Port Arthur, the journey of the convict ships or the areas of London where Ikey lived will be covered by location shooting.

There is also a virtual treasure trove of contemporary art work and graphics of the period, and extensive use will also be made of these to convey the atmosphere of the time.

Production Setup

The film is being produced by Fury Productions of Australia. The very highly experienced production team responsible for the film includes Producer Veronica Fury (Fury Productions), Alan Rosenthal (Writer-Director), Helen Gaynor (co-director), Consultant Leslie Woodhead (England).

What I tried to do in the above proposal was convey four things to a would-be producer:

We had a good story.
It was a story that had elements that would appeal to a broad public.
We had a strong and very interesting central character.
It had plenty of physical action and personal conflicts.

DOES THE SUBJECT ATTRACT YOU?

Once you choose to write about a certain subject, you'll probably spend at least three months to half a year on the case. That's a big chunk of your life. Why do you do it? Well, it could be the appeal of the money, which I well understand, and that's a very solid professional reason for writing. It could be that the subject fascinates you, and you believe it would be fun to write about it. Again, not a bad reason. But beyond both those solid reasons I believe that it often helps to hold a belief in the need for your film, and the good that it might do. This comes from my upbringing in British social documentary and is a distance away from American docudrama entertainments.

In *Who Bombed Birmingham?*, the writer, Rob Ritchie, set out to show that the wrong men had been convicted in a British murder case. In *Hillsborough*, the writer examined, for the first time, the possibility of police culpability after a 1989 disaster at a British football stadium, in which ninety-five spectators were crushed to death.

In an article he wrote for the *Guardian* newspaper in England, my friend Michael Eaton, a top-flight concerned scriptwriter, put the driving motive this way:

> There are two responsible kinds of docudrama. One attempts to review contentious, problematic moments of our collective public history. The clarity of dramatic depiction is mobilized in a way that conventional documentary cannot be, in order to expose hidden injustice.
>
> The second type, however, tries to shine a beacon onto some apparently well-known case, to delve beyond the surface of newspaper headlines. It needs to pick away at some terrible aberrant social sore that somehow reveals the working of the society we have all carded up to.

Michael presents an ideal not all of us will aim for, or want to emulate, but his thoughts are very useful to keep in mind.

PART TWO
STARTING TO WORK

4. RESEARCH

Research is the master key to fact-based films, and you undertake it with two objectives in mind. You are looking for facts, and you are trying to get to the heart of the drama. In order to write your script, you must know your subject in depth, inside out and upside down. Only when you really know the subject will you be able to see where to go: how to shape the film, structure it, select the dominant characters, create an interesting story line, and so on. Research provides you with your lexicon of options.

As a researcher, you need to combine the penetrating brazenness of the good journalist with the painstaking attention to detail of the PhD candidate. You must be observer, analyst, student, and note taker. Over a period, which can be as short as a few weeks or as long as six months or a year, you must become an expert on the subject of your film, a subject you may never even have known existed before; not easy, but always fascinating.

Research can be broken down into four sections: (1) print research, (2) photograph and archive research, (3) direct interviews, and (4) on-the-spot involvement with the subject, or location research. In practice, you are likely to be involved in all four forms of research at the same time.

PRINTED MATERIAL

Within sensible limits, you try to read as much as possible about the subject. This is particularly true of history-based docudramas. Your aim is simple: within a short time, you want to become, if not an expert in the field, at least a person with a superior knowledge of the subject. So print research can involve scanning major bibliographies and subject biographies and reading papers, magazines, trade and technical journals, articles, diaries, letters, even congressional records and trial transcripts.

If the material is highly technical, complex, or jargonized, you should get someone to help you so that the material becomes comprehensible.

The BBC series on the life of nuclear physicist J. Robert Oppenheimer dealt, on a superficial level, with fission theory. Not an easy task for a researcher, but it had to be tackled and made comprehensible. Again, Michael Baker's script on the *Exxon Valdez* oil disaster involved lengthy research on the development of the Alaskan oil industry, and the complex measures for pollution control. Again, an immense amount of material had to be assimilated and understood before Michael could work on the script.

Another problem is that much of the material may be out of date or presented from a biased or self-serving point of view. When I think that the material comes from a biased or highly partisan source (particularly in films of a political or controversial nature), I try to check the biases of the informant as well. I also double-check statistics, remembering the old adage "There are lies, more lies, and statistics."

One point is of supreme importance, certainly in investigatory docudramas. Try to go back to original sources for your information. Don't be content with second- or third- hand reports. If you are doing a film about a character or incident in World War I, don't just read a few history books. Instead, start digging out documents, wills, diaries, and contemporary newspaper accounts. In films about government policy, you have to dig into official records, state papers, memoranda, and the like. Not easy, but very necessary.

Newspapers

Besides suggesting stories as subjects for docudramas, newspapers and magazines can often provide a lot of the basic research and background detail for the subsequent film. In the notorious Amy Fisher case, NBC and CBS both used participants in the original dramas as their principal sources of information. Excluded from that process, ABC based its account very largely on newspaper reports and court records.

Although newspaper accounts can be very useful, they often have to be taken with a grain of salt. Are they accurate? Are they sensationalist? Can they be believed? How thorough was their research?

After a while, you learn to discriminate. You might suspect a yellow journalism crime story, but if it appeared in *New York* magazine, then the odds are it has been meticulously researched and the facts checked. But not always, and even top journalists can be biased and sloppy, and jump to immediate conclusions, as in the *Costa Concordia* story.

What one also looks for in a newspaper, besides facts, is the feel and atmosphere of a time and a place, or the way a particular community reacted to a particular story or incident. This can also be very helpful where there has been no original TV coverage.

Google

Using Google, or another search engine, can also be useful for giving you a first handle on a story. It can point you to biographies and sources, but has to be used very carefully. Wikipedia, the free encyclopedia, for example, is often compiled by anonymous contributors and cannot be taken as the gospel truth.

Freedom of Information Papers

A problem facing many researchers is they suspect the information is there but they can't get their hands on it. In the private sphere, there is often little that can be done. If someone doesn't want to release an intimate diary or letters, that's it. Or if a company doesn't want to release its memoranda, one may just have to accept the situation. However, things are slightly different in the realm of information held by the government on individuals. Such a case may well be covered by the 1977 Freedom of Information Act.

As a result of this act, interested parties can gain access to information collected about themselves or well-known individuals by the government. This ability to open previously and jealously closed doors proved vital in the research of films such as *JFK*, *Chaplin*, and *J. Edgar*.

The act also proved useful in the preparation of the Robert Oppenheimer series for the BBC. Peter Goodchild, the series producer, told me the following:

> Initially the problem seemed to be how to breathe life into Oppenheimer and make him less of a totem. We needed to find more about his personal life and relationships. Here we benefited from the new Act. The reports we uncovered showed how continuous the surveillance of him was. It showed how he had been propositioned by Chevalier and others, and that the prosecution counsel at the hearings had tried to get the FBI to intervene when he thought the panel was swinging in favor of Oppie. In a nutshell, we really felt we had got something of an inside track.

Books

Books also provide you with enormous research potential but also have to be absorbed with caution. When I was researching the life of Ikey Solomon for my film *The First Fagin*, I came across a book that told the stories of several Australian convicts, including Ikey. Subsequent research showed me that much of the material on Ikey was pure invention.

Where a sole book is the principal source for your film, like Tom Wolfe's *The Right Stuff*, about the U.S. space program and especially its astronauts, you may have to be careful of the book's accuracy. Less wariness may be needed if your brief is merely to adapt the book "as is" and forget anything else. This was the course followed in adapting *The Longest Day*, about the invasion of Normandy, and for *Young Winston*, about the Boer War adventures of Winston Churchill.

One of the staple offerings of docudrama is the biopic, and in many cases the biography or autobiography becomes the chief source. But often, as in the case of Hemingway, van Gogh, Churchill, and countless others, there could be three or four good biographies, and the researcher has to pick his or her way through the best of them.

The problem comes when books are in dispute and viewpoints radically different. For example, one of the most provocative books out on Frank Sinatra is *His Way* by Kitty Kelly. The book is fascinating and deadly, and a very unpleasant picture of Sinatra emerges from it. Quite clearly, it could have been a fascinating basis for a controversial, but not necessarily truthful, docudrama. However, the series on the singer eventually made by Sinatra's daughter presented a basically positive view of Frank, with Kitty Kelly's views being almost totally ignored.

Diaries and the Like

We hunger for revelations and inner secrets, and the juicier and the more lurid, the better. And in searching for what is concealed, we turn to the diary, whether written or videotaped. We do this because we know that if the writer can't bury his or her hidden passions, fears, hopes, and devils in the confiding secrecy of the diary, then there's probably nothing worth burying at all.

In the end, we turn to diaries, not only out of a thirst for scandals or a whiff of sexual impropriety, but also in the quest for something much more serious. We know that if the journal or the diary is honest and reasonably accurate, we can get a glimpse into the inner life, thoughts, frustrations, and dreams of our subject.

The diaries can be very old or very recent. Darwin's journals helped form the basis of the British series on the pioneering naturalist. Freud's notes, diaries, and letters helped enormously on the writing of the series on his life. When Leslie Woodhead made a film on Soviet dissident General Grigorenko, the very basis of the film was provided by Grigorenko's detailed diaries, which he had managed to smuggle out of prison.

Diaries can be a wonderful tool . . . up to a point. One has to remember, however, that they are often written with an eye on posterity, and with a view to historical self-justification. This is particularly true of political, military, and literary journals. They may be fascinating, but are they truthful? Well, that might be something else again.

Court Transcripts

Sometimes, in my more cynical moods, I find myself wondering whether dramadocs could exist without what now seems to be the inevitable court scene that provides the climax to so many films.

Digging into case transcripts is going to be one of those research jobs you are going to have to face, sooner or later. It may be tiresome work, involving a great deal of reading, but it can also be quite fascinating, and in many cases absolutely necessary. This is not just because of the search for truth and accuracy but comes from the fact that in most cases the trial record is more dramatically fascinating than anything you could invent.

Today, what we see most often are trial scenes in murder recreations, but trials and trial-like confrontations are quite often used to address much wider issues in the docudrama.

In *Stanley and Livingstone*, the Society of British Geographers meets to judge the maps that prove that Stanley could actually have found Living-stone. In *The Mountains of the Moon*, the same society sits in judgment on the rival claims of Burton and Speke to have found the sources of the Nile. In the Canadian Film Board's *Democracy on Trial: The Morgentaler Affair*, the whole film rests on Dr. Morgentaler's three trials for running an abortion clinic in Montreal.

The power of trial transcripts can also be seen in Leslie Woodhead's *A Subject of Struggle*. Woodhead's film is about an elderly Chinese woman put on trial by the Red Guards at the height of the Cultural Revolution. In 1972, when the film was made, the nature of the revolution was a tremendous enigma, and no film of any worth had come out of China about it. Woodhead obtained the trial transcript, talked to sinologists about it, and the used the transcripts as the basis for his film.

PHOTO AND ARCHIVE RESEARCH

The need for photo and archive research arises most frequently in history-based docudramas. This kind of research can give you three things:

The feel and look of a period, whether it be the 1960s or the 1930s
An understanding of your main characters, their habits, their appearance, and their actions
An understanding and insight into certain key events that are necessary for your film

Often you will be looking at the archives as both a source of inspiration and as actual visual material that can be incorporated into the final film. The assassination of Kennedy in *JFK* is possibly the simplest example.

Your sources for photographs and stock footage are fairly obvious. In the usual family/incident/injury/murder docudrama such as *Friendly Fire*, *Afterburn*, *Little Mo*, or the Amy Fisher films, your materials will probably be obtained from the subject's family or friends, and from their private albums, attics, and old video cassettes.

In regard to historical and political films, your sources may be more complex. Depending on your film, you may be searching government archives (such as the British Imperial War Museum, or the National Archives in Washington, D.C.), local and press archives, or television archives. The last, for example, were used very widely in *Citizen Cohn*.

Once you have a general source for your material, you may still find it difficult to locate what you want. Archives are often arranged haphazardly, and though many have been computerized, a few archives still use index cards.

INTERVIEWS

In films on contemporary subjects, much of your time, maybe even most of your time, will be taken up in fieldwork. Either you or your researcher may have to get out and conduct multiple interviews to collect the facts for your film. Your objective in direct interviews is to talk to as many "experts" on, or participants in the subject as possible. Again, as in print research, you may have to make some judgments about usefulness. Since time is limited, you try to assess which people are the best, the most important, and the most open, and you allocate your time accordingly.

When Granada TV made *Hostages*, a docudrama about hostages in Lebanon, Alasdair Palmer, the associate producer went out and interviewed returned hostages, such as Frank Reed, and friends, such as Jill Morrell, who were working for release of their loved ones. Similarly, when Simon Chinn was making the Channel 4 film *The Government Inspector*, about British weapons inspector Dr. David Kelly, he and his researchers worked for eighteen months and conducted 120 interviews. So you have to be prepared to sweat it out.[1]

Today, a high percentage of TV docudramas revolve around the sudden, bizarre incident happening to an ordinary family or the next-door neighbor. What complicates the situation is that the major subject will now often talk only after the payment of large sums of money.

In the Amy Fisher case, the Fishers allegedly collected $80,000 from KLM productions for film rights, which meant exclusive interview rights. Against this, the Buttafuocos got over $200,000 from Tri-Star for their version of the same story.

When HBO wanted to make a film about Wanda Holloway, the scheming mother in a Texas would-be murder case, they eventually paid Mrs.

1. For further analysis of research methods for docudrama on British TV, see Derek Paget's chapter "Working in Docudrama" in his book *No Other Way to Tell It: Docudrama on Film and Television*.

Holloway's former husband and her daughter $130,000 for joining in the deal and telling their story. They also paid Verna Heath, the intended victim, $50,000 for her recollections.

What is clear also from the above is that money pays for a specific point of view. You pay for and interview the husband and daughter of a murdered woman, then your story will probably favor their point of view. Pay for an interview with the murderess and her lover, and the story will be biased in different direction.

Outside these domestic dramas, what kind of interviewees are you looking for? Usually those most deeply involved in the subject. They can range from technical experts and authorities to the ordinary people who have undergone the experience you want to document in the film, such as people who were in the Twin Towers in a film about the 9/11 tragedy, or safety officials and the miners themselves in a film about the Chilean mining disaster. In brief, your perspective and the breadth of your subject will dictate to whom you talk, and your questions will obviously range from the general to the specific, depending on the topic.

Occasionally, the interviews can alter your first perception of the story and lead you in a totally different direction. This happened to Antony Thomas, writer and director of *Death of a Princess*. The film deals with the events leading up to the public execution of a Saudi Arabian princess for adultery and actually caused a rift in British and Saudi Arabian diplomatic relations when it was first broadcast. Thomas told me the story of his research as follows:

> I presented the idea to ATV. They were interested, and off I went, only to discover that the research was utterly baffling. I discovered very early on that many elements of the story I had been told were simply not true.
>
> The most solid lead was that the Princess was supposed to have met her lover at the University of Beirut. So I felt I should begin in Lebanon, and find the people who had known her, who had taught her, who were her classmates. . . . Then came the shock. After two days in Lebanon I discovered part of this wonderful dramatic story was nonsense. The girl had *never been* to the Arab University of Beirut.
>
> But I soon discovered something else very interesting, that the girl had become some sort of mythological figure in the Arab world. She had become both a personal and a political symbol, and everyone was adopting her to their cause. Thus for a Palestinian family she had become a freedom fighter. So this ability in the Arab world to deal in myth, hearsay and legend took off after the Princess. I was slow, but gradually I began to see the importance of these elements.

Approached correctly and sympathetically, most people will be willing to talk to you for your research. Occasionally, however, you will run into difficulties, for instance, if the subject is professionally damaging or controversial. Thus, it was no surprise to the researchers in the Lockerbie disaster film to find that both Pan Am officials and German airport authorities were reluctant to talk to them. In this case, a former policeman, with no fear about job security, and former employees of Pan Am helped break the logjam.

What if the subject is personally painful or the events bordering on the criminal? Do you go ahead, or back off? Everyone has to sort that dilemma out personally. Several years ago, I interviewed Susan McConnochy about a film she was doing on war criminals. I was interested in her difficulties in talking to former Nazis for the film, because she was investigating not just memories and experiences, but also possible participation in war crimes and atrocities. Her comments were very interesting.

> Initially it was quite difficult to get people to open up. However, once the Germans agreed to see you and talk it was all much fresher than the English people's reminiscences because it hadn't been told before. . . .
> But once I got in a position of trust it was an almost impossible situation. The reason was I was dealing with people who, in the period of their lives that we were talking about, had not operated with the same code of behavior, morals, or whatever you call it, that I by nature and upbringing operate on.[2]

Reliance on only a few interviewees concerning anything controversial has its dangers. In such a case, as with the *Exxon Valdez* oil spill, it's best to try to interview a very broad range of people. This way, you can contrast opinions and estimate how much of what you are being told is biased or partisan.

Obviously, you have to rely on common sense. You are not aiming for balance; you are trying to get at the truth; and it could be that the one-sided view just happens to be the truth.

During the interviews, you will ask both the easy and the awkward questions. Sometimes, you may have to play the probing investigator, but more often you are asking commonsense questions that any interested person would bring up.

In a technical film, for instance, one on the *Exxon Valdez* catastrophe, you may want to accumulate facts, and find out about a ship's engineering problems, and systems of work. In a biopic, or portrait film, you will probably want to find out about people's experiences, memories, changes, and

2. Alan Rosenthal, *The Documentary Conscience* (Berkeley: University of California Press, 1980): 69–70.

thoughts, and about the consequences that certain actions have wrought on peoples' lives.

Often, the interviewing will be difficult or painful, as you touch on emotions and sensitivities. You are not just collecting facts but trying to gain a perspective that goes beyond facts. An adjunct to this is that you always have to keep in mind whether you want the emphasis to fall on facts or emotions, because each may pull you in a different way.

LOCATION RESEARCH

Much of your research will be done on location. While one of your objectives is to get to know your characters, an equally important goal is to get a feel for the background and the atmosphere of your story.

In order to write his film about the *Exxon Valdez* disaster, Michael Baker had to spend months in Valdez, Alaska, observing all the details of the town and the way the oil industry worked, and, not least in importance, getting a feel for the beauty of the town.

Before writing *Shoot to Kill*, the true story of the deliberate killings of IRA members by special police units, author Michael Eaton spent weeks soaking up the atmosphere of Belfast and other Irish towns.

The list is endless. The point clear. If you the chance to see where everything happened, then go there. The experience will make all the difference to your writing.

RESEARCH IN PRACTICE: AN EXAMPLE

In 2012, I made a historical docudrama for ZDF Germany, and for Australian television, (and the proposal of which I outlined earlier). The film was called *The First Fagin*, and this is how it came about.

One evening a few years before, I was having dinner with my friend Helen in Melbourne, Australia. She'd just come back from a holiday in Tasmania and told me an interesting story. She and her husband, Arpad, had visited a small jail in a town called Richmond, which 150 years before had housed a Jewish English convict called Ikey Solomon. The point, according to legends in the jail, was that many people thought Ikey was the template, the original model, for Fagin in Dickens's *Oliver Twist*. Immediately, the light bulb went off in my head. Could there be a film here?

That night, I Googled everything I could find about Ikey Solomon. His was an amazing story. He'd been raised in London in the early 1800s, had married Ann when he was very young, and had become a pickpocket. After being caught by the police, he was sentenced to serve time on the Hulks, the old warships along the Thames that served as floating prisons. On release, he quickly prospered and became the richest, most successful receiver of stolen goods in London. But, again, he was caught by the police and this time sent to Newgate, London's oldest jail. Here, he staged an amazing jailbreak and fled to America.

This incident caught the attention of the newspapers and pamphleteers, and Fagin became the most famous criminal in London. Anxious for revenge, the police framed Ikey's wife, Ann, and she was sentenced to fourteen years transportation to Van Diemen's Land (now Tasmania). Out of love, and madness, Ikey then sailed from the America to Hobart, Tasmania, which was then a penal colony. Ikey very quickly found his convict wife, who was working as a housemaid, and set up shop. After being joined by two sons, he was ready for a new life.

Unfortunately, George Arthur, the governor of Van Diemen's Land, thought otherwise. After he seized Ikey, a trial ensued in Hobart, to see if Ikey could stay legally on the island. Notwithstanding a verdict in Ikey's favor, he was hijacked, and sent back to England, where he stood trial for theft at the Old Bailey. After a guilty verdict, Ikey was again sent to Van Diemen's Land, this time as a convict, and served time in two of Van Diemen's Land most notorious jails, including the Port Arthur penal colony.

So it was quite a tale, and I saw three lines to follow for a possible docudrama. First, we would look at and tell Ikey's dramatic personal story. Second, we would investigate the nature of crime and punishment in England and Australia in the nineteenth century. Finally, we would investigate whether Ikey really was the model for Fagin, Dickens's rascally Jewish fence, receiver of stolen goods. But to do the film well required immense amounts of research, and below I've set out the main sources I turned to.

Books and Written Materials

Ikey and Ann's letters (Tasmanian archives)
Old Bailey, Tasmanian, and New Norfolk court records
Newgate prison archives
The First Fagin, a biography of Ikey by Judith O'Donnell Sackville
Prince of Fences, a biography by J. J. Tobias
Van Diemen's Land, about convicts in Van Diemen's Land, by James
    Boyce
Closing Hell's Gate, about Macquarie penal colony, by H. Maxwell-Stewart
London Life and the London Poor, by Henry Mayhew. This is a classic
    study of London poor and social conditions around Ikey's time and
    was invaluable
The Criminal Prisons of London, by Henry Mayhew. This equally fine
    volume by Mayhew was my main source of information about life in
    the prisons and on the Hulks

Dickens and Crime, by Phillip Collins
Three sensational cheap pamphlets on Ikey's life and escape, including
   The Life and Adventures of Ikey Solomon

In addition to the above, I read a lot of novels about English and Australian convict life, including the classic *For the Term of His Natural Life*, by Marcus Clarke.

Graphic Materials

The sources here seemed endless. For example, I trolled the archives of East London Museum, the British Museum, the English Maritime Museum, and the Tasmanian National Archives for starters. Then I looked at the illustrations in Mayhew's books, and in Gustav Dore's *London*, and searched antique bookshops in London for volumes with illustrations of the period. Finally, I started looking up old periodicals like the *Illustrated London News*.

Google's image search was quite useful for finding old illustrations. Here, one had to be careful because, though the illustrations gave a good idea of the atmosphere, many could not be used in the final film because of copyright claims that would be very expensive to clear.

Of course, what is absent from the above is any mention of photos, one of the most common sources for research—but not in this case, for one obvious reason. Though Niépce had done some pioneer work in 1826, photography didn't really take off until after the experiments of Daguerre and Fox Talbot in early 1840s. So photography couldn't help us.

Location Research

The two areas for research were obviously London and Tasmania. The former unfortunately proved disappointing. For example, Newgate prison had been torn down, and the original Old Bailey law court had also been demolished. Ikey had lived in London's East End, close to the old Petticoat Lane market. But that too had changed out of all recognition, the area having been taken over by high-rises and up-market condominiums.

Tasmania, the new name for Van Diemen's Land, was much more promising. Many of the old buildings, courts, and houses had been preserved, and much of the countryside looked exactly as it had in Ikey's day. So here I armed myself with pen and notebook, cajoled a friend to drive me around for a week, and went hunting. The results were good. Ikey's jail at Richmond was still pretty well preserved and yielded up atmosphere and detailed facts about Ikey's life.

The Port Arthur penal colony was good, but not quite as useful. There were a number of old prison buildings, but Ikey's original compound was gone. Nevertheless, the whole area had not changed very much physically. There was still the sea, the jetty, and the dark surrounding woods, and with a stretch of the imagination we could easily envisage what Ikey must have seen every day of his imprisonment.

Armed with all this information, I then went back to my computer to start writing. Part of what emerged can be seen in chapter 7.

SOME PRACTICAL HINTS

Although research itself is largely a matter of patience, application, and common sense, there are a few practical tips that may help you along the way.

Identification

People you visit, see, or write to want to know who you are. Get yourself a business card that identifies you and also gives your address and profession, such as "Tom Marks, scriptwriter and film producer." Also get yourself some well-printed stationery that says the same thing, or use well-designed, personally addressed paper. And if you're working for a producer or production company, make sure you've got their stationery as well.

Payments

Many libraries and archives are free, but there are a good number of others that demand payment for use of their facilities, by the day or by the hour. Specialized services in free libraries may also ask for payment and most definitely will for all photocopying. So take a credit card and plenty of cash.

Interviewing

When you want to get a foot in the door, you use whatever method fits the situation. If you are interviewing a public figure, then a phone call to his or her secretary mentioning your interest, followed by a letter will probably do the trick.

When you are dealing with a private person in the public eye, things may be trickier. Here, you try to find out as much about the person as you can before making contact. If the person is shy of reporters, then try the low-key approach. If she or he is hungry for publicity, then you drag out your NBC or BBC credentials and jump in there.

The Sequence List

What is very important is that as you proceed with the research, you make yourself a sequence chart that shows when events occurred, and who was involved in the events. You'll find this chart helps you enormously when you come to write the film and keeps you on track as to who did what, to whom, and when.

5. The Dramatic Elements

You've found your subject. It looks commercial. It has audience appeal. You've done your research, and you think you're on to a winner.

You've got a good story. It's about an attractive person with whom the audience can identify, caught in a threatening life crisis. You've got villains. You've got complications. You've got twists, surprises, and a certain amount of humor. You've also got a lot of physical action. Your hero goes through a lot of reverses but eventually comes out fine.

You have all the essentials of a good script. So how do you proceed? By planning and considering structure and development. Before you start writing you need to know exactly where you're going, with whom, and at what speed, and roughly what's going to happen along the way.

It's also useful to write out for yourself a one-line sentence expressing the essence of the film. "*The King's Speech:* this is about a man, who aided by a most unlikely opposite character, overcomes immense personal and family problems to inspire his nation at its time of crisis."

The procedure is a little like building a house. Unless the architect gets his design and plans right, the building will be a mess. Exactly the same is true of scriptwriting. In your case, the whole framework and success of your script depends on the fusion and cohesion of four vital dramatic elements:

Story
Conflict
Structure
Character

There are, of course, many other factors in the script that are going to be important, including dialogue, atmosphere, tension, surprise, humor, pacing, and beginnings and endings. Most of these topics are dealt with in the next chapter. However, important as they are, these subjects can be discussed only when you've got the main elements settled in your mind.

THE PROBLEM OF REALITY

You're ready to jump in—but hold it. Isn't there a basic problem here we haven't discussed? Discussion of all the elements we've mentioned is fine, but this book is about fact-based dramas, tales drawn from real life. It's about situations already given to us, conflicts that are already to hand, characters who have an existence apart from our computers, stories that don't yield easily to ideal theories of structure. Do the same dramatic criteria apply to this genre? And even if they do, how do you impose these elements on a *found* or given situation?

The answer to the first question is a simple "yes." The elements of drama are universal and exist as much in real life as in fiction, if not more so. The real question is the second one. How do you create an interesting form and a compelling dramatic structure out of fascinating but often muddled, seemingly shapeless, and complex real-life events? And how do you do it when your creative stretch is constrained by truth. In short, as a friend of mine put it, writing docudrama is like boxing with one hand tied behind your back.

The solution is to gain a broad understanding of the main elements of drama, and then to focus this knowledge on your real-life situation. Your work then becomes a sifting process. First you have to identify all the elements that have a potential to be in your script: interesting characters, fascinating situations, major and minor conflicts. You have to recognize themes that will involve your audience, events that will progress the story, possibilities for subplots, potential action scenes, and incidents that reveal passions at their most extreme.

What you find become your raw materials. You then measure them against your dramatic criteria. That's when the juggling, sifting, eliminating, and arranging process starts. Slowly, you try to work out story development; the appropriate structure to carry the movie; evolution of the conflict; and interaction of your characters. Get the relationship of these things correctly balanced, and you are halfway home.

Story, conflict, characters, structure. These are the elements that drive your script forward. These are the elements that provide the framework and backbone for everything you do, and you must get them right. So your first job is to review your research, and see how the material you've gathered relates to the above four subjects

STORY

In this and the following three sections, we're going to examine the basic dramatic elements a little more closely, and see how they unite in constructing a good script. To make things a little more interesting, I've occasionally chosen fiction films as illustrations when I think they provide very clear examples of the problem under discussion.

The first problem is to find a good story, and in chapter 4, we already discussed many of its necessary elements, and the basis of a story's appeal.

What is one of the standard stories? We take an interesting character and usually present him with a goal or a mission. We present him with a series of problems on the way; and the manner in which he overcomes the problems, or succumbs to them, gives us the body of the story.

We call the action, or the unfolding of the story, the plot. Some films, like *JFK*, will have elaborate plots, densely packed with surprises, twists, and reversals. Others, like *The Queen*, with Helen Mirren, may have a very simple plot, with few twists. And then a TV film like *The Life and Death of Peter Sellers* may be the simple telling of a picaresque life.

Your first task is to decide *what* kind of a story you are dealing with. Research has shown you a story with many possibilities that could go in all directions. Now you must find its main premise, its strongest underlying element, as I mentioned before, the one sentence that guides you through the film. Thus, my guiding line for *The First Fagin* was "We are telling a passionate love story that ends in disaster." Yes, it was also a story of crime and punishment, but it was the love story that gave it its backbone.

Most stories, but not all, resolve themselves into one of three types:

Goal oriented
Issue oriented
Journey and transformation

Goal-Oriented Stories

Two good examples of goal-oriented stories are *The African Queen*, directed by John Huston, and *The King's Speech*. In the first, the goal is the blowing up of a German ship in the First World War. In the second, the goal is to cure the new king's stammer. Both are fairly simple stories, with marvelous characters, but while the first has many plot twists, the second is much more straightforward.

The goal-oriented story line also pervades many docudramas. In *Willing to Kill*, the goal of Wanda Holloway is to make her daughter the school's top cheerleader. As that general goal gets more and more frustrated, her goal narrows down to the killing of her daughter's rival. In *Death of a Princess*, the goal of the journalist Paul is to discover the true story behind the killing of the young Saudi Arabian girl. In *Barbarians at the Gates*, the goal of the hero, Ross Johnson, is to take over one of the largest companies in the U.S. *Game Change*, about Sarah Palin's campaign for vice president, can also be seen, in a sense, as a goal-oriented film.

Issue-Oriented Stories

Many films take their inspiration from issues of public or general concern. In *Erin Brockovich* for example, Erin fights a West Coast gas company on the issue of deadly local pollution. Usually, this kind of film sets up the issue, and the unfolding of the plot shows you how the issue was solved, or how it affected people's lives.

Issue-oriented films are particularly attractive for docudrama, and public problems and concerns have provided the basis for some of the best films in the genre, such as *And the Band Played On*, about AIDS, and *Skokie*. Ernest Kinoy's script for *Skokie* dealt with a neo-Nazi march to take place in a suburb of Chicago that stirred up immense public controversy. Here, the issues were freedom of speech versus the wounded sensitivities of a large group of the public.

Across the Atlantic, Granada TV's *Who Bombed Birmingham?* dealt with the imprisonment of six men falsely accused of blowing up a Birmingham public house. Here the film actually helped to bring about the release of the men.

Stories of Journey and Transformation

Many films find their main interest in character transformation as their heroes journey through life. This is the key element that underpins *Gandhi*, *Malcolm X*, *The Social Network*, *Erin Brockovich*, and *The Life and Death of Peter Sellers*.

We are interested to see how the main character behaves during the process of transformation. Thus, Peter Sellers starts his life as a modest, happily married, small-time actor and gradually turns into aggressive, bullying star. In Peckinpah's *Straw Dogs*, Dustin Hoffman plays an American mathematician living in a small English village. He is presented at first as a mild, cautious man who cannot act even when his wife is raped. Later, he gives a mentally retarded man refuge in his house, when the latter is being hunted by a local gang.

When his house is subsequently attacked, Hoffman goes wild and in a series of brutal sequences succeeds in killing or maiming most of the gang. This possibility of transformation from weakness to strength is hinted at throughout the film. When it happens in the final sequence, the effect is devastating.

Now, looking at stories in terms of goals, issues, or journeys is obviously simplistic. On the one hand, many of the elements can often be found in the same story, and on the other, such a listing can in no way cover the multiplicity of story elements. Nevertheless, simple or complex, the essence of the matter is that you must very quickly find the underlying premise of your story. It may be one of the above types. It may be something else entirely, but you have to identify it. Once you've found it, you can begin to think how to tell yours story, and what all the incidents, events, and twists are that will make it exciting, dramatic, and entertaining.

It may help to make a simple list of some of the essential points. Ask yourself, What is the issue that underlines my film? What are the goals of my main character? If he or she changes, how do present that change? The items you have on your list may never openly appear in your film, but your answers are going to be the subtext that drives your film, or the pillar of fire that lights your way.

CONFLICT

Without conflict, there is no drama. Conflict means confrontation and is the key element of your film. Without it, you are lost. Without it, you have no story, or no story that will interest an audience.

Conflict is that element that stands between you and your goal. It's the barrier, the opposition, the hurdle that prevents you realizing your aspirations. It's denial of your needs, your dreams, your hopes.

Sometimes, the conflict is physical or external: John Wayne against the Mexican troops in *The Alamo*, David Koresh against the FBI in *Ambush in Waco*, or Margaret Thatcher against her detractors in *The Iron Lady*. Sometimes, it's internal, as in *Oppenheimer*, where the physicist struggles with his doubts about unleashing nuclear warfare. Sometimes, it's cosmic: the Children of Israel versus God in *Moses the Lawgiver*.

Conflict requires an opponent. It may be nature itself, as in *Nanook*, *Touching the Void*, *127 Hours*, or *Alive*. More often, it may be a simple villain. It may be the other suitor of the hero's wife. It may be Governor Arthur, who wants Ikey put in jail in *The First Fagin*. It may be the forces of society. It may be big business. And the opponent or the opposing force comes in many forms, not always evil. In *Diana: Her True Story*, Diana's opponents are not just the royal family, but also tradition and societal norms.

Occasionally, the opponent is time itself. The Chilean miners are fighting to survive as their air runs out. It was another battle against time that underpinned *Lorenzo's Oil*, where parents try to beat the clock in finding a cure for their dying child.

The element of conflict is also never considered alone. Once you start thinking about conflict, you also have to consider its relationship to *needs*, *goals*, and *action*, and their revolving interplay within the script.

Your hero needs to sing. His goal is to become the best singer in America. His parents reject the idea. Here, already, are two opposing forces at work. *Action* is needed to resolve the conflict and satisfy his needs. Your hero leaves home. He rises in the music world and then wants a particular job. Someone opposes him. Once more conflict. Action is now needed to overcome this drawback as well. He bypasses the opponent, goes for a secret audition, and wins the job. Such is the basic scenario for a dozen films, ranging from *The Jolson Story* to *Sinatra*.

What one sees on further analysis is that there is often one long-term goal, and also a series of intermediate minor goals: getting the job, winning the girl, getting into television, and so on. Barriers are set before each goal, requiring a response or action from the hero. And so the film proceeds through challenge and response to the final reel. Conflict is the key, and it is your character's response to the conflict, or barriers before his goal, that gives you the substance of your film.

In the same way that you made a list of your underlying story issues, it is also worth listing your conflict points, both major and minor. You can set this down in various ways. I find the simplest way is to list things as follows:

Conflict or dilemma	Action taken	Consequences
Bill Gates wants IBM job. He doesn't get it.	He goes out alone.	Creation of Microsoft. New computer world.
Mark Zuckerberg's girlfriend sees him neglecting her. He ignores that.	She leaves Mark.	He attacks her on a new campus website.
Diana can't get love and attention from Prince Charles.	Throws herself down the stairs.	Charles furious. Royal family becomes more antagonistic. Marriage worsens

Besides noting the action taken, you must also note the consequences. They can be minute or far reaching, and they are often totally unexpected. In *Pirates of Silicon Valley*, Bill Gates's decision to concentrate on programming leads to the birth of the age of the personal computer. However, Princess Diana's act of throwing herself down the stairs, contrary to expectations, worsens her relationship with Charles.

Hero and Villain

This is the standard conflict in most action films. Characters are simplistically presented with clearly clashing roles. In *The First Fagin*, Ikey wants to live in freedom in Van Diemen's Land, but Governor Arthur passionately wants him in jail. In *The Raid on Entebbe*, the hijackers holding the hostages are the bad guys, and the Israeli soldiers who effect a rescue are the heroes. Most courtroom films are also set up on this simple hero-villain premise. Thus in *Erin Brockovich*, Erin is the heroine battling for human rights, and the polluting gas company the villain of the piece.

Inner Conflict

Here, the elements begin to get more interesting and more subtle. Often, the hero or heroine is faced with a moral dilemma. The path of action and resolution is far from clear, and the audience becomes fascinated by the hero's decisions and indecision.

In *Citizen Cohn*, lawyer Roy Cohn's father begs him to give up helping Senator McCarthy and support the cause of liberalism. The conflict here is between the father's path of decency and the allure of fame and self-aggrandizement. In *The Queen*, Queen Elizabeth is torn between maintaining a cool monastic reserve regarding Diana's death and joining the country in an expression of mourning.

In *My Week with Marilyn*, Colin Clark's dilemma is whether to stay with a sick and seductive Marilyn Monroe, or obey the order of his film boss and keep his distance and his job. Here, the allure of a seductive Marilyn solves the problem for him.

Relational Conflicts

These types of conflicts form the basis of most screen romances and love stories. The usual goals of the couple are romance, sex, love, and possibly marriage. But the clash of personalities and the different minor needs, goals, and aspirations of each of the pair make for a series of conflicts that bar the way to happiness.

Excellent examples of this kind of conflict can be seen in all the films about the British royal family, from *Fergie and Andy: Behind the Palace Doors* to *Charles and Diana: Unhappily Ever After*. If one prefers an American perspective on relational conflict, then there are the numerous films on the Kennedy family, including *A Woman Named Jackie*.

Societal Conflict

This conflict usually pits one man or woman, or a group, against a larger group or organization. The opponents can be family, the tribe, big business, bureaucracy, the government, even the country. The issues at stake are usually not money, but status, tradition, justice, corruption, and progress. Two examples that show this conflict very clearly are *Friendly Fire* and *Afterburn*. Both of these highly rated films tell similar stories of families battling the government to expose the truth about the death of a son or husband during military service. In *The Iron Lady*, Margaret Thatcher fights old Tory political diehards to show that a woman can in fact become leader of the Conservative Party.

A fourth example, *Diana: Her True Story*, appears on the surface to be a Cinderella story gone sour, or a story about falling in and out of love.

In reality, it's a story of a major societal conflict, with a young girl totally opposing tradition as embodied by the most powerful family in the land.

The Complications of Conflict

While we appreciate that conflict is needed in a good script, problems can arise in putting theory into practice. One mistake is to present too many conflicts. So many hurdles are placed in front of the hero that we lose interest. We know (at least in fiction) that he is going to prevail in the end, so after a while we cease caring whether he faces another villain. This was almost the problem of Harrison Ford in *The Fugitive*. As it happens, the film was saved by the intricacy of the plot twists and some excellent directing—but it was a narrow escape.

Your script is also at risk if you present unequal protagonists and antagonists. When one of your main characters is always stronger, brighter, and swifter than the other, then much of your conflict goes down the drain. That's why the Superman and Batman stories were neglected for years as film material. They just weren't interesting until the development of special effects placed the focus elsewhere, off the man and onto intense action.

STRUCTURE

The finest piece of advice ever given to scriptwriters is to be found in William Goldman's book *Adventures in the Screen Trade*. Goldman, a gifted writer of over fifteen major scripts, including *Butch Cassidy*, says it all in three words: "Screenplays are structure." As he puts it, "Nifty dialogue helps one hell of a lot. It's nice if you can bring your characters to life. You can have great characters spouting swell talk to each other, but if the structure is unsound, forget it."[1]

For a scriptwriter, structure is framework, form, and modeling. By structure, we mean the sound shaping of a story. It is the solid underpinning that will carry the story from page 1 of the script to the end. Structure is about order, and how to arrange your real-life story in the best possible way. It tells you where to place your sequences, events, and major and minor conflicts, so that your film becomes as powerful as it can possibly be. Structure is also about finding the strongest beginning, middle, and end for your film.

The form most commonly used in fiction films is called the *three-act structure*, or three-act design. In this system, each act serves a different function. It's a concept that has been around for hundreds of years and is discussed in detail below. The three-act structure doesn't cover everything, but it's a useful notion for the writer to hold in his or her head.

---

1. William Goldman, Adventures in the Screen Trade, 460.

The problem is that the story or the events in your docudrama may simply not fit in to this classic mode. The unfolding of real-life drama, as we know, is very different from fiction. Nevertheless, some of the ideas below may be useful to you, and helpful to bear in mind as you proceed.

Act 1

Act 1 sets up the premise. It can last twenty to thirty minutes in a screenplay of an hour and a half and has to grab or hook the viewer. If you can't do that, your film is dead before it's gotten off the ground.

Act 1 lets you know who the main characters are and the problems they face. It usually tells you about the background of the hero, introduces his or her main antagonist, and hints or tells you directly about the main conflict or basis of the story. It's the catapult mechanism that shoots the plane off the carrier. It sets up the action and gives the story direction and a strong push to get it going. Act 1 ends when you have set up very clearly the predicament facing your hero. Then comes act 2, providing the complications.

In *The King's Speech*, act 1 introduces the problem of a stammering Prince Albert, who cannot speak in public, and his meeting with his possible savior, speech therapist Lionel Logue. By the end of the act we have also met the prince's wife, Elizabeth; an unlikable King George V; and a playboy brother, Prince Edward. In *The First Fagin*, act 1 introduces us to Ikey, a well-known London fence, who's served time in jail, and has escaped to America. It also introduces Ikey's wife, Ann, and the rest of her family. Here the act ends with Ann being sent to Australia as a convict, leaving Ikey with the dilemma as to what to do.

Act 2

Act 2 contains the mass of your story. This is the section where complications set in and multiply. Here the hero gets deeper and deeper into his predicament. Often, his goals seem harder and harder to achieve. There seems to be no way out. And the twists and turns of the plot keep multiplying.

Let's look for example at a fictional film, that great comedy *Tootsie*. As the second act progresses, Dustin Hoffman (1) succeeds in becoming the nation's top woman TV star, (2) falls in love with Jessica Lange but can't reveal he is a man, and (3) is himself pursued by both a male TV actor and Jessica's father.

Act 2 is always about compounding the problems, putting on the pressure, and providing more complications and barriers. In *The Kings Speech*, act 2 covers Logue's unorthodox methods in curing Prince Albert (the future King George VI) and looks at Edward's abdication from the throne and the increasing speech challenges to the new king. It ends abruptly when the new monarch accuses Logue of treason and dismisses him from his service.

In *The First Fagin*, the second act shows Ikey joining his wife in Van Diemen's Land, a British penal colony. The complication to what should have been a quiet new life is the fact that the martinet governor of the island, George Arthur, is gunning for Ikey. The section the ends with Ikey being thrown in prison, and then sent back to England to stand trial for theft at the Old Bailey. The suspense is raised because we know Ikey could be hung for theft.

Act 3

Act 3 brings all the loose strands together. It solves all the problems and provides the resolution. If act 2 lasted fifty minutes, act 3 it likely to last twenty or thirty minutes. It tells us what happened to the main characters, how they solved their conflicts, and how they overcame the various barriers.

In Ikey's case, he is found guilty in a highly publicized trial, is sent to a terrible penal colony, and, on release, finds his wife has betrayed him with another man. Not a happy ending, but that's what occasionally happens with true stories. In *My Week with Marilyn*, the final section shows Marilyn almost seducing Colin, completing her film, and flying off into the sunset. Meanwhile, Laurence Olivier swears never to direct another film.

DOCUDRAMA DIFFERENCES

While plays and standard movies often fit neatly in to the three-act formula, that's rarely the case with real-life stories. They are usually much more jumbled, complex, and convoluted than simple fictions. Because of that, it often helps to think of your film, particularly a biopic, in terms of a linear chronological progression, marked by key emotional and life highlights. Before writing *The First Fagin*, I jotted down a few of Ikey's life highlights as follows: prison on the Hulks; freedom and happy marriage; prison and escape to America; decision to follow wife to Australia. These highlights provided a guide for the first part of script. However, I also kept in mind that that the key point to be stressed was Ikey's decision to follow his wife to Australia, although he was still a wanted man.

In *Infamous*, the story of Truman Capote's writing of *In Cold Blood*, the key points are Capote's decision to go after the story, the refusal of the local police to give him access at first, and the attempted rape of Capote by one of the murderers. In Scorsese's *The Aviator*, the emotional highlights follow each other in fast succession. Hughes's first successes as an inventor; his entry into film; his affair with Gloria Swanson; his dream of an airline; and his obsession with cleanliness. The emotional marks and career highlights are very clear, providing clear guidelines for an interesting script.

The simple linear progression for a biopic was the standard method used in the old Hollywood biography movies. Very often, however, the structure became formulaic and clichéd. One would see the inventor, singer, musician, or writer at the start of his career. No one would believe in him except his wife. After battling the dark night of the soul, he suddenly succeeds. His invention, song, rhapsody, or novel is praised by the world. He gains fame and fortune, takes up with loose women, and loses his wife. In the final act he sees where love and duty lies and rejoins his family.

Well, this formula worked for a hundred or so films, but my advice is to leave it alone.

Further Considerations

The seven-act structure. Television drama differs from motion pictures in two important aspects that affect you as a writer. First, whereas the feature film can be any length, from say an hour and a half to two hours, a docudrama on a U.S. TV network at prime time is usually written in two-hour segments. This really means about one hundred minutes a show, after allowing for commercial breaks.

A second point, and a consequence of those commercials, is that the drama is usually constructed in *seven* acts instead of three, with four of them coming in the last hour. Obviously, the writing is geared so that there is a climax plus a question mark at the end of each act so that the viewer will be hooked, and will resume watching when the commercials are finished. Another thing to note is that you should aim for a high point at the end of the first hour, as viewers often change stations on the hour, and you want to keep them with you for the remainder of the film.

Tidiness. Sometimes, the three-act structure or seven-act TV structure seems too neat, too tidy, too artificial. Life isn't set up in such a simple way, and as I've already mentioned, that structure may not be right for many docudramas. All this is true, but you have to remember that structure is not a rigid framework. You play with it in the way that best suits you. It's a starting point when you are unsure of your techniques and capabilities, and it's a tremendous help even when you're experienced.

These ideas on structure are not gospel. They are not a set of rules written in stone. The three-act structure is merely a guide that seems to have worked for filmmakers from D. W. Griffith and Anita Loos to William Goldman, Lawrence Kasdan, and Joe Eszterhas.

Pace and acceleration. Structure gives you the basics, the order of your scenes, and the development of your plot, but for the film to work, the scenes have to be paced. The viewer has to be drawn in more and more deeply. The rhythm has to quicken. One has to become more and more involved, and concerned with what is at stake. In slang, you have to up the ante.

Most of these things we'll deal with later, as we work through treatments and adaptations, but start thinking about them now. Without them, your

neat structure will remain lifeless. Add these elements, and your script will
live and breathe.

Action points. Most scripts depend on two or three major incidents or
happenings to spin the plot in a different direction at a crucial moment of
the script. Often, they are referred to as plot points, or turning points. I
prefer to call them action points. These action points serve many purposes:

> They propel the story into the next act.
> They refocus the drama.
> They raise the stakes.
> They demand major decisions and actions by the hero.

In *The King's Speech*, the main action point is when Prince Albert (Bertie)
decides to engage Logue as his speech therapist. In *The Changeling*, the
turning point is when Christine (Angelina Jolie) is forcibly put into a mental
health ward for denying that the boy delivered to her is her son. Another
major action point occurs when detective Kelly reveals that Northcott murdered thirty boys, possibly including Christine's son. In the classic film *The
Fugitive*, the key moment comes when hunted convict Harrison Ford makes
a decision to hunt for the real murderer of his wife.

And so it goes on. You keep asking yourself what are the important
questions to be faced and resolved before you start the script. Gradually,
you see that the two most important are going to be:

> Is my structure clear?
> Are my action points correctly positioned to work for the film in the
>   strongest way?
> If you can say yes to both, you are in a good position to proceed.

The sequence. Each of your acts is going to be made up of various sequences. These are units of the film, connected by place, idea, or action.

In *The King's Speech*, the first sequence introduces Prince Bertie. Subsequent sequences serve to introduce his family, his speech problem, his
"quack" helpers, and his possible savior in the form of Lionel Logue. In
The Changeling, two key preliminary sequences reveal that Christine's son
is missing, and that a local minister is attacking the LAPD for corruption.
These are the set-up sequences. They are quickly followed by two vital sequences where the police claim to have found Christine's son, Walter, only to
have that claim and her "son's" identity denied by Christine. These sequences
set up the main thrust of the film—Christine versus the L.A. police boss.

Within the overriding arch and premise of your film, you are constantly
searching for interesting sequences that will hold your audience all along
the way. Sometimes, they are sequences of tension, such as the life and death
struggle of a climber at the start of the Sylvester Stallone film *Cliffhanger*.

At other times, they are sequences that prove the wit and fame of the hero, such as the bantering scenes with Truman Capote at the start of *Infamous*. Usually, the opening sequences start with a bang, but not always. Thus the rather slow starting sequences of *The Iron Lady* are there to show her advancing illness. Normally, this would have been a turn-off, but the start is saved because we know we are going to get a biography of one of the most famous and accomplished women in the world.

Your aim is not just to make the sequences funny, tense, or dramatic in themselves. They have to do more. They must show us something important about our protagonists, and they must advance the story. In other words, each sequence must have a clear *function* that you should be able to plot. All this can be seen very clearly in the first few sequences of *The King's Speech*.

Sequence	Function
Prince Bertie's dressing room. Royal dress uniform on bed.	Introduce pomp of royalty, and Prince Bertie.
Broadcast studio. BBC.	Set up tension for Bertie's broadcast.
Wembley stadium broadcast. King, and politicians present. Bertie stutters in broadcast.	Introduce Bertie's speech problem.
Elizabeth, Prince Bertie's wife, visits Logue's office.	Attempt to find cure for stammer.

The way sequences work can also be seen in the example below, where I've analyzed the development of *Barbarians at the Gates*. The film deals with the problems of the tobacco firm RJR Nabisco, as company manager Ross unsuccessfully tries to market a new smokeless cigarette, and improve stock market ratings.

Sequence	Function
1. Ross and wife in limousine going to company party.	Give atmosphere of sex and luxury. Introduce Ross.
2. Party at Nabisco headquarters.	Show luxury style of company execs., and introduce secondary characters. Life is fine as TV shows cancer smoke trial fails.
3. Ross and others execs. talk between private planes.	Reveals problem. Stock price low. Reveals new cigarette is planned.
4. Tennis club. Fancy occasion.	Shows that shareholders are worried. Management buyout now seen as an answer to the company's problems.

Once we finish with introductions and background, we get into the problem (sequence 3). Sequence 4 offers a solution that will lead to complications. Besides driving the plot forward, each sequence emphasizes the tantalizing baubles of money, glitz, and luxury—temptations that bewitch everyone in the film.

When you write your own films, try to follow the examples above. List your possible sequences, and describe their functions in the plot. When you insert something for a purely technical reason, say to advance the plot, ask yourself whether it's really interesting. Overall, this shorthand process reveals immediately the point and purpose of the sequences, or whether they are just there for padding.

CHARACTER

A script is not often about an idea or a place. It's about a person whom we usually like, who gets involved in a crisis or complex situation. Sometimes, the crisis is of his or her own doing. Sometimes, it's a crisis precipitated by someone else, which gradually involves the hero. The hero takes action, and the plot gradually thickens, until the last act resolves everything.

So who are our heroes?

Larger Than Life

In many films, we require our heroes to be larger than life. We want them to be able to do things we only dream about. We want to live vicariously through their courage and their actions.

Fiction scriptwriters are aware of our needs, and to satisfy us they give us Batman, Rambo, and James Bond. When writers of docudrama want to do the same thing, they often turn to history and give us Lawrence of Arabia, Patton, Eisenhower, and films like *Band of Brothers*.

Like Us but More Determined and Fascinating

When we tire of the great heroes, we search for characters with whom we can identify easily. We want them to be like us so that we can empathize with their plight, and yet their lives should be a little more interesting and compelling than ours.

In *The Changeling*, we admire telephone supervisor Christine Collin's determination to find her son, and are then appalled by her treatment at the hands of the LAPD. In *Erin Brockovich*, we have the epitome of an ordinary working-class woman who gets fired up to save a community.

Sometimes, the stories don't end happily. Thus, except for one man, the heroes of *The Flags of Our Fathers*, who planted the U.S. flag on Iwo Jima, go from fame and fortune to poverty and drunkenness.

Fascinating Villains

There is one rule every scriptwriter knows. If you have to choose between telling the story of a saint or a sinner, take the sinner. The story of Mother Teresa may uplift you, but the lives of Hitler or Stalin or the story of Bernie Madoff or Kahn Strauss will give you better ratings. Thus, what impelled me to tell the story of Ikey Solomon was that he was a thief, a receiver of stolen goods, and also a man who ruined his life for love.

The rule about going for sinners is particularly applicable to television and docudrama. In most years, it's the movie with the best villain or the best sinner that tops the ratings. *Citizen Cohn* told the story of Roy Cohn, the henchman of Joe McCarthy. He was an utterly detestable character, yet he was so compelling, one couldn't move away from the TV set. Similarly, in *The Changeling*, the scheming, career-obsessed head of the LAPD gives us a wonderful contrast to Angelina Jolie's Christine.

Character Dimensions

To be interesting, your characters must have dimensions. They must have aspirations and goals, needs and demands, virtues and defects; and on the whole, they must be real and believable. Above all, they must have a certain magnetism or charisma that makes us interested in their plight. To a certain extent, that is provided by good casting, but the basic qualities must be there in the way the characters are written. We must be able to empathize with them, and we must be concerned about them. If we are not drawn to them, if we are not fascinated by them, if the characters leave us cold, we don't have a film.

Motivation

We are going to follow your hero for an hour or so and watch him or her get in and out of various scrapes. He's going to act and react, and we must know why. We must understand the basis for his actions. We must understand what motivates him. Is it greed, power, survival, sex, love, or revenge?

When the motives of all your characters are clear, the film proceeds very easily. If you forget motivation, your script will begin to leak like a sieve. This was one of the faults of ABC's *Willing to Kill*.

The real-life movie traces Wanda Holloway's obsession with getting her daughter on the school's cheerleading team. The obsession is so strong that she is willing to take out a murder contract on the mother of her daughter's rival. This is fascinating in its own way until we begin to ask why: Why would a woman go to such extremes to get her daughter on the cheerleading team? It's a critical question, and the film never quite answers it.

THE ELEMENTS COMBINED

What I've presented up to now is a survey of the key elements in your script, from story through character. I've tried to get you to think about their use in a logical way, and to see how each element relates to the others. But I realize there is a danger of making everything too schematic, and films aren't made that way. There is no such thing as writing by numbers. However, analyzing the key elements allows you to really think about what you are doing before getting down to the real work. The process helps you organize your thoughts and suggests areas that you ought to consider before you commit yourself to the actual script.

6. SHAPING THE TOTAL DRAMA

After considering the elements of story, conflict, and character, you still have a few questions to answer before tackling the script. Your concern is how to shape the film into a logical and emotional whole. Here, you are concerned with problems of approach, framework, attack, and rhythm. You are taking another look at structure and form but from a slightly different angle.

APPROACH

Writers tell stories in different ways. Some simply go from A to Z. Others tell the story in flashbacks. Others use the outsider who views the events from a distance. Whatever the method used, the writer has to define his or her basic framework before writing a word.

Your challenge is to tell the story in the most interesting manner. Most TV productions use a simple linear and chronological approach. This is the form most frequently used, because it satisfies our natural curiosity to see what happens next.

If we are introduced to the gifted kid who sings all day, we want to know what happens to him as an adult. We know Stalin ruled half the world, so let's see how he got there after an insignificant beginning. We see Mark Zuckerberg as a nerdy student and want to see how he gets on at Harvard and develops Facebook. And we want to see how Bill Gates and Steve Jobs came from nowhere to build two empires.

Chronology gives us a chance to observe process and growth. It enables us to understand how incidents in a career, home tragedies, and professional obstacles shape and form our main characters. Seeing where they come from, and what they had to battle against, we appreciate the final triumphs even more.

The simple linear approach is also the attack most used in films dependent on crisis, conflict, and resolution. Thus, in *Everybody's Baby: The Rescue of Jessica McClure*, we simply follow the rescue of a baby who has fallen down a well. Again, in *United 93*, we see the preparations of the terrorists before they board United flight 93, the plane in flight, and the receipt of information by the passengers of the Twin Towers disaster, before we conclude with the passengers' battle for the cockpit before the plane crashes.

The chronological approach is simple and effective and usually gives us a good story with a defined beginning, middle, and end. But there are many variations, and some of them can be quite effective.

Parallel Stories

A fairly common approach to narrative form is to tell two stories at the same time. They are usually about the same person, but one story takes place now, and one story is set in the past. However, as the current story proceeds, our understanding of the actions and character of our "hero" keeps changing, as more and more information is revealed about the past.

This "then and now" approach dominates the structure of Michael Eaton's docudrama *The Enemy Within. Enemy* tells the story of Michael Betteny, who worked for MI5, the British internal security agency, and offered his services to the Russians. In the end, Betteny was caught and sentenced to twenty-five years in jail.

I asked Michael to give me the rationale for his structure.

> Now remember, the public knew a lot about the story. They knew that there was an MI5 officer who had passed over secrets. So I decided to enter from there. I decided the best way to do the film was to start the story at the moment of his decision to give information to the Soviets.
>
> So, as it were, there was a *present* to the story, a *now* to the story, from the time he decided to give the secrets to the time he was caught. That made it into a kind of thriller structure. Finding out there is information being leaked, and tracking it down.
>
> But at pertinent moments of this *now*, there were flashbacks into the *then*, into the past. We would see Michael at the time of his recruitment into the service. We would see him serving as field officer in northern Ireland. We would chart his growing disillusionment, his inner anxiety, and the turmoil that made him take this dramatic step. The *now* of the thriller story was also being set against the past. This helped shed light on the institution of MI5 and also on his motives for betrayal.

This question of time frame was one I also had to consider very seriously in a film I wrote about the British Sinai explorer Edward Palmer. The facts of Palmer's life are fascinating. He was a nineteenth-century Cambridge don, or university professor, and one of the greatest linguists of his day. With the support of the Palestine Exploration Fund he went to the Holy Land in 1868, then under the Turks, and spent a year exploring the Sinai desert.

He returned to England to great acclaim, and wrote a best seller about the strange Sinai wilderness. In 1882 he set off once more for the Holy Land to do further explorations, and also to spy on the Turks for the British government. When he disappeared in the desert, a rescue party was sent after him under the leader ship of Captain Charles Warren. But Palmer was already dead, murdered by Bedouin tribesmen, who were caught by Warren, tried by him, and hanged in among the sand dunes.

My problem was to find the proper attack and entry into the story. On the surface there were two obvious approaches: (a) tell the story chronologically; (b) start with the trial and then relate the events that lead up to Palmer's death. Neither approach satisfied me.

The problem with the chronological approach was that we had a slow beginning—Palmer in Cambridge, Palmer the Don—till we got to the more exciting part of the film, which was the first Sinai trip. This meant that in a TV movie about an unknown British explorer, people might well move to another channel before the story hit its stride.

Starting with the trial had the disadvantage of giving the whole game away. Assuming there was a mystery in Palmer's disappearance, and a mystery that would fascinate an audience, we would be wasting our best dramatic shocks too early in the film.

My ultimate solution, with which I was very happy, was to start the film with a British search party under Captain Warren going out to hunt for Palmer. This gives you a search, a goal, and a mystery right at the beginning. The audience then wants to know who *is* this man you're looking for, and you retrace Palmer's story. Eventually *past* catches up with *present* as we discover the murder and the mystery is solved.

Experiments with Form

Many filmmakers think there is a standard pattern for writing scripts. Nonsense! What should dominate your thinking about form and style is that there is no prescribed, hallowed way of writing fact-based drama, or for that matter, any drama.

For starters, give your approach a bit of freedom. Remember, the only boundaries are those of your imagination. I know the form used in most films and TV movies is straightforward, realistic, and prosaic, but think for a moment. You could opt instead for fantasy, humor, farce, or parody if you believe that approach or style would make for a more interesting or successful script. A simple example here occurs in *Pirates of Silicon Valley*, where a character jumps out of board meeting, violating the fourth wall to talk directly to the TV audience.

In the classic film *Citizen Kane*, writer Herman Mankiewicz and director Orson Welles have great fun playing around with form. They take Kane's story and then examine it and reexamine it from four or five different angles, as the story is told and retold by different characters. The film uses black humor. It uses realism and expressionism and plays around with the editing. It takes chances, and it works.

These kinds of experiments also surface in Antony Thomas's docudrama *Death of a Princess*. In Thomas's film, we are presented with a problem. A reporter knows a Saudi Arabian princess has been executed. But why? And who is this girl who brought such a drastic punishment on herself? The questions haunt the reporter, and to answer them he embarks on a journey of discovery. Eventually, half a dozen characters all give a different version of the truth, exactly as in *Rashomon*.

One of the best examples of experiment in form is undoubtedly the series *The Singing Detective*, written for the BBC by Dennis Potter. In *Detective*, Potter tells the story of a mystery writer who is hospitalized with a painful skin disease. It doesn't seem like a great subject for a series, but some regard it as the best thing ever done on British TV.

First of all, Potter plays around with past and present. So we see the writer in hospital, and also flashbacks of him as a child. After that, Potter takes off into the realm of fantasy, giving us slices from the writer's novel. To complicate things further, Potter breaks out of realism and has his characters sing and dance to the pop music of the 1940s. It is an experiment which in lesser hands could well have crashed on takeoff. Piloted by Potter, the drama soars off into clouds of applause.

Hybrids

Though most of this book is devoted to writing the docudrama in standard form, that is to say using actors, dialogue, and dramatic reconstructions, for years writers have played around with variants of the form. Many of these variations do not depend on the truth and take liberties with the usual techniques. Most of the variants fall into three categories:

Dramas suggested by news events or pressing social conditions
Dramatic sections within straight documentaries
Dramas using multiple documentary techniques and sections

Dramas suggested by news events. The most famous examples in America of dramas suggested by news events were the TV plays put out by CBS's *Armstrong Circle Theatre* between 1950 and 1963. The stories were often based on or inspired by newspaper headlines and current events dealing with drugs, crime, and so on, but they used fictitious names, fictitious locales, and imagined actions and consequences.

The same technique was often used in England, but on a more sporadic basis. Thus Tony Parker won fame for a number of very authentic and realistic TV dramas based on interviews he had conducted with prison inmates about their lives, habits, past actions, and conditions.

At the same time, Jeremy Sandford was writing *Cathy Come Home*, about the lives of the homeless, based on a series of interviews he had conducted for BBC radio on the subject. The characters and the actions in the final film, directed by Ken Loach, were fictitious but based on real people and real incidents. The film had an immense impact on the public, who acknowledged the authenticity of its origins, and it helped alleviate the poor conditions for the homeless in the U.K.

Docudramas within documentaries. The last ten years has seen an increasing use of a film approach whereby half the film is documentary, the other half a dramatized reenactment. Here, the two most famous examples are *Touching the Void* and *Man on Wire*.

Touching the Void was made in 2003 by Kevin MacDonald. It recounts a nearly disastrous climb of the west face of the Siula Grande mountain in Peru by Joe Simpson and Simon Yates in 1985. During the climb down the mountain face, Simpson broke his leg and was slowly lowered down by Yates holding the upper rope. When Simpson slipped over a cliff edge, and began pulling Yates toward the abyss, Yates had no alternative but to cut the rope; otherwise both would have fallen to their deaths. Miraculously Simpson survived and wrote a best-selling book about the catastrophe.

In MacDonald's film, half the story is related by the real Simpson, Yates, and a third climber, just telling their stories simply and frankly in front of a curtain backdrop. Often, however, their talking serves as voice-over for dramatic reconstructions of the climb and accident, filmed in various mountains with breathtaking audacity. It all works wonderfully well, with the film receiving top prizes around the world.

Incidentally, this technique of the dramatic personae acting in and retelling their own stories has been used in a number of films. For example, it was used in Jack Gold's *90 Days*, made for the BBC. Here, Ruth First relates her experience of internment in a jail in South Africa during the apartheid period. She also plays herself in the reenactment. I also used this method in an early docudrama of mine, *Special Counsel*. In this case, an American lawyer relates and replays his experiences acting as an intermediary between President Carter and President Sadat in the Camp David accords of the late 1970s.

Man on Wire is a 2008 Oscar-winning British documentary. It tells the story of Philippe Petit's hair-raising high-wire walk between the Twin Towers of New York's World Trade Center in 1974. For the most part, it is standard documentary, mostly using old film clips, interviews, and still photos. However, the key part of the film deals with the arrangements of Petit's team to secretly gain access to the towers, bring in their gear, get to the roof, secure the security blocks for the walk, and actually string the rope between the towers. Here, the film uses very successful black-and-white dramatized sequences. They work extremely well, and without them the film would have been impossible. In one sense, the whole reenactment reminds one of a heist movie, and with that in mind, we relish the drama.

Dramas using documentary techniques. In recent years, more and more docudramas have been made essentially incorporating many documentary techniques, beyond those discussed in the preceding paragraphs. Here, I'm referring to interviews, narration, and substantial use of still shots and archive material.

One example of this can be seen in *Letters of a Bomber Pilot*, an extract from which appears at the end of this chapter. In *Letters*, we get extensive narration and are also provided with an interview with Bea, the film hero's wartime girlfriend. Another good example is the 2006 *9/11: The Twin Towers*, coproduced by Dangerous Films and Blakeway Productions for the BBC, ATL, France 2, and Discovery. This too mixes acted scenes, archives, and witness statements in order memorialize that disaster day.

The use of documentary materials is also a device I employed for about 20 percent of my *First Fagin* film. The reason was simple. One of my sponsors, German television, had asked me to tell the viewers a great deal about crime and punishment in the England and Australia in the nineteenth century. This could not be done via the simple story of my hero. Instead, I had to use narration, experts, and a lot of graphics. This was actually quite simple to do, but the main problem was then integrating the documentary material into the main drama story. Eventually, we did this quite smoothly, but it wasn't easy.

The Holocaust on Trial, made in 2000 by British director Leslie Woodhead, is another very interesting example of the use of a hybrid form. The film is an examination of the libel suit brought in 2000 by historian David Irving against Holocaust expert Deborah Lipstadt. It also briefly outlines some of the history of the Holocaust. At first, the film seems to be using a standard documentary form, using archive material to give the viewer a background on Irving, and the lead-up to the trial. However, it then uses dramatic reconstruction to give us the highlights of the trial itself. The amazing thing, and a tribute to the director, is that having seen the *real* David Irving in the archive pictures, we also totally accept the actor's portrayal of the same person.

Beginnings

You have your form (standard or experimental), your characters, your incidents, and your conflicts, but how do you begin your script. The opening of the film has to do two things very quickly. First, it has to catch, or "hook," the viewer's interest, and second, it has to define what the film is about and where it's going. These are good artistic rules, and also good practical rules in a world where your films will primarily be seen on television and have to compete with many other programs for viewers.

The only real exception to these rules is when you are dealing with a very well-known, totally presold subject. In *The Iron Lady*, about Margaret Thatcher, the beginning was quite slow, but it didn't matter because we knew we were about to see the portrait of an incredible character.

The opening "hook" should play into the audience's curiosity. You present an intriguing situation, and you say, "Watch me! You'll be fascinated to see where I'm going to take you." So the curiosity is piqued, and the imagination stimulated. We want answers to our questions, so we decide to stay with the film for a while, but only so long as there is a payoff from the first few shots. They had better be leading somewhere interesting.

Following this approach, this is how I started my script of *The First Fagin*:

The First Fagin: [abbreviated opening]

We are in Newgate prison. A subtitle tells us it's London, May 1827.

1: CU on jail bars and a massive iron door. CU of boots coming along a corridor.

A door is unlocked with massive keys. We pull out to see two warders and a convict.

The iron jail gate is unlocked. The warders pull the convict outside. A dark street is seen through thick London fog. The jail door is shut and bolted.

2: The outline of a hackney cab and horses is seen through the mist. We tilt up to see the cab driver's face wrapped in a scarf.

3: The horse drawn cab clamps down the cobbled street. Inside the coach the two jailers lie drugged, twitching and unconscious. The convict raps on the inside roof of the cab. It stops. The convict jumps out, and the cab driver unlocks his handcuffs, and gives the convict a hat and scarf. The two men embrace, and the convict runs off.

NARRATION

When Ikey Solomon—a dealer in stolen goods—masterminded his own brazen escape from custody, the public was enthralled. Ikey, as he was popularly known, was facing charges of theft, and a possible hanging. Now, the most notorious criminal suspect in England was on the run, showing up the British authorities as total fools.

Here there is the drama of an escape, but also the questions How did he do it? And how come the warders are drugged? The hope is the viewer will go on with the film to get the answers.

Bernard MacLaverty's film *Hostages*, about the hostage crisis in Lebanon, also catapults into action from the start. Here, the film opens with a news montage illustrating the chaos and anarchy of Beirut in the mid-1980s. Bombs are exploding. Gunfire is heard, and a news voice-over says, "When the fighting reaches its fiercest, Beirut looks like hell on earth." Immediately after that, we see the abduction of Terry Anderson and Tom Sutherland. You are, as they say, in with a bang.

Antony Thomas's *Death of a Princess* starts a bit more slowly, but what it lacks in speed it most certainly makes up for in fascination and in capturing your curiosity.

Death of a Princess. Sequence 1

A vast construction site. Eddies of sand go by. An open air café lashed by the wind . . . a flapping tent . . .

A convoy of vehicles (crushed tight by a long lens) dips and turns in the desert.

Flat roofs. Narrow alleys. It is the time of prayer. The market empties for worship. Prayer is heard from a dozen mosques.

The convoy of vehicles approaches through the desert. Three cars. Two covered vans. Details of three veiled women through limousine glass.

Three European workers in a jeep are stopped at a roadblock . . .

Congregation at prayer in mosque.

A pickup truck dumps a pile of sand in the market square.

Crowd comes out of the mosque. Construction worker fights his way through the crowd. Strains for a good view.

The vehicles of the convoy are in position in the car park, at the centre of restless spectators. An old man with a sword and scabbard kisses a dignitary.

Van doors are unlocked. Two figures stumble out. A veiled woman in black and a 22-year-old man. Two soldiers lead the woman to a pile of sand and force her to kneel.

6 men sit on the spokes of a giant wheel, motionless.

The construction worker hurries away from the crowd. Freeze on his face. Six pistol shots gradually die away.

Montage of headlines and press photos. "Girl Shot for Love;" and "The Boy Who Wooed her Executed by the Sword."

It's a hypnotic beginning, the suspense building as we gradually realize what is going on: that we are going to witness an execution, a ceremonial death. At first, the details are deliberately blurred: the convoy is seen in the distance; everything is a little hazy. Then it becomes clear, and we are horrified at the implications of the scene, and the indifference of the spectators.

Again, as in my *Fagin* film, certain questions are set up, with the promise that they'll be answered later in the film.

If your film is about some charismatic figure—a historical personality, a famous singer, a champion athlete—it helps to introduce these characters early and hint at the conflicts surrounding them. You can surprise the viewers, and let them know they are going to see sides of this well-known character they never even dreamed about.

In his script for the TV series *Stalin*, Paul Monash needs to get us into the film, but also show us a facet of Stalin that will intrigue us. How does he do this? By showing us a brief scene at the Imperial Military Headquarters, where Stalin is being examined by a doctor before army induction.

The first lines of the doctor tell us that Stalin is thirty-eight, is called Joseph Vissarionovich, was born in Georgia, and was exiled to Siberia for revolutionary activities. This information is put over in a fairly quick, painless, and not too obvious way. But the doctor's next remarks really surprise us.

DOCTOR
Conscript has the following deformities. Left arm two inches shorter than right, possibly congenital defect . . . Second and third toes of left foot webbed and joined, skin pockmarked.

OLD MAN
The mark of the devil!

OFFICER
Rejected!

This really shocks us, that Stalin, who supervised the battle of Stalingrad, was rejected by the army. Who would have thought it? Interesting! This scene is immediately followed by one telling us that the tsar had abdicated, and we are into the body of the film without any wasted time.

The first remarks of the doctor, telling us where Stalin comes from, are short but relevant. They help us get over the problem of *backstory*. By backstory, we mean the information the audience needs to know about what has happened before the film started, so that the events of the film make sense.

Providing backstory tends to be a problem, and there are ways of solving it subtly or crudely. Crude backstory might go as follows, with the information spoken by a character:

JOHN
Ah, Richard. Aren't you the new boy from Australia? They told me you were very rich, your father was a banker, your mother had died, and that you were a tennis champion. I also heard that the girls adore you.

A more subtle way of presenting the same information might be through visual clues that might be described thus in a script:

> *Richard gets out of taxi. He gives the driver thirty dollars, thinks, then adds another twenty for tip. As he carries his case upstairs, the maids look him up and down in sexy approval. In his room he takes off his jacket and we see his black arm band. He quickly arranges tennis photos, Australian pennants and a few trophies. He finally arranges his family photos, parents, brother, sisters, and the hardest one, the single shot of his mother.*

You can reveal backstory by dialogue, but my own preference is to reveal it by action. The same thing applies to character depiction.

Throughout your script, you will be telling us about your characters through their dialogue and by their actions and reactions. However, we need to know fairly quickly at the start of the film exactly with whom we are dealing, so that we can get a fix on the characters.

The very first scene in *Stalin* shows him shooting a rabbit and dragging it off, leaving a trail of blood. The message is clear, a bit obvious, but maybe necessary for TV: that Stalin is going to be soaked in blood all his life.

In William Goldman's *Butch Cassidy and the Sundance Kid*, Sundance is introduced in a very funny early scene. A card game is going on, and Macon, the saloon keeper, accuses Sundance of cheating. Sundance denies this but says if he's invited to stay, he'll go quietly. Macon refuses and seems intent on a shoot-out. Butch keeps begging Sundance to back down and tells him he's over the hill. Macon might be good. He might be very fast. Butch tells Macon the two of them will behave if he asks them to stay. But Macon gets bolder and bolder, until Butch says, "Can't help you, Sundance."

Utterance of the name "Sundance" changes the direction of the scene. Macon realizes he's facing the finest gunman in the West. He backs down and abjectly asks Sundance to stay. It's a very funny reversal, but the scene hasn't yet reached its climax. This happens when Macon says, "Kid, how good are you?" On this, Butch jumps for safety as Sundance whips out his guns, shoots off Macon's gun belt, and puts three bullets into it as it snakes across the room. Then Butch and Sundance leave, with Butch's parting words being, "Like I've been telling you . . . over the hill."

When writing is as good as Goldman's, it moves from art into ecstasy.

RHYTHM AND PACE

A good beginning to takes you into a film with a bang, with a sense of expectation. The problem then is how to sustain interest through the next hour, through the second act. Most of the problem is solved if you've provided yourself with a solid structure, interesting incidents, and a fascinating plot. Even so, there will be pitfalls, and many of them have to do with *rhythm* and *pace*.

What do we mean by good rhythm and pace? Quite simply that a film should have a logical and emotional flow, that it's level of intensity should vary, that it shouldn't drag and become boring, that it should hold our interest all the time, and that it should build to a compelling climax. Unfortunately, it's easier to point out the problems than it is to offer all-embracing solutions. Here are just a few of the most common problems:

Sequences that go on too long
Lack of connection between sequences
Too many similar sequences following each other when we thirst for variety
Too many action scenes and too few reflective scenes
No sense of development or logical or emotional order to the sequences

Are there any hints about rhythm and pace? First, *get into the film quickly.* Establish what you're going to do, then do it. Second, *build the film with variety between the scenes,* and a gradual crescendo of climaxes. By crescendo, I mean the *intensity* of your crises and problems. The confrontations and difficulties should probably be small at the beginning of the film but of major consequence at the end.

Where you have to modify some of the above ideas is when you come to write TV dramas, and have to allow for a two-hour, seven-act structure and the disruptive effect of commercial breaks. Here, your need for sequence variety stays the same, but your films are probably built up of a number of smaller crises, rather than evolving to one grand finale

This can easily be seen when you look at the old Sinatra miniseries for CBS. Instead of one major drama, the series proceeds through a variety of challenges and confrontations, such as:

The young Frank versus his family
Frank's struggles for his first singing jobs
Frank's battles with band leader Tommy Dorsey
Frank's wife versus the other women in his life
Frank's battle over Ava Gardner
Frank's battles with his studio

Each story is sufficiently interesting to sustain us for fifteen minutes of screen time, until the commercials, and then we gradually move on to the next incident. Here, in the Sinatra series, we are not looking for much more than a few good songs and some compelling scenes from a widely lived life.

If there is any one point that needs stressing, it's the need for variety in the type and tempo of the scenes you're writing, and *Butch Cassidy* provides excellent instruction on the issue. *Butch Cassidy* was one of the most successful "buddy" movies ever made. A lot of the success was due to Goldman's superb sense of structure, and to his marvelous feeling for variety and tempo.

The film is full of sequences of action, pursuit, and gunslinging, but Goldman knows even these can get boring. So in the midst of things, he inserts an idyllic scene of Paul Newman bicycling with Sundance's girlfriend among the trees, while the song "Raindrops Keep Falling on My Head" plays. It's a light, funny scene that allows us to breathe and relax before we return to the chase. The love of bicycles, incidentally, is a detail faithful to the historical Butch Cassidy.

Rhythm and pace are in many ways the most difficult things for a beginning writer to handle well. One of the reasons is that they are such nebulous and insubstantial concepts. Yet they are two of the secrets of good screenwriting.

One of the most effective methods to help you with the problem is to make a simple graph of your script. You then plot the rise and fall of the action and confrontations as points on a curve. You should arrive at a picture of mountains and valleys, with the mountains getting higher and higher as you proceed toward the climax. If your graph gives you a straight line, or a very gently modulating line, you are probably writing a bedtime story rather than a James Bond movie. If your graph gives you a roller coaster, then you've probably written an action movie with few letups.

Another thing you can do is mark your action scenes in red, and quiet or contrasting scenes in blue or green. This will give you a quick visual picture of the contrast in moods in your film. When you've charted both the action and the moods, you should be able to spot very easily where the problems lie in the film.

You can work out endless variations on this idea of graphing the script. You can plot when characters come in, you can star the turning points, and so on. That's all useful but has to be taken with a warning. If you are not careful, it can reduce scriptwriting to a very mechanical formula, whereby technical data is fed into the computer and the script emerges. That's the way to hell. However, the graphing of climaxes and moods can be of some assistance in the beginning. If you have a problem, try it out and see if it helps.

ENDINGS

We all know what should happen in the ideal ending. There should be a big climax, and then maybe a short scene before fade-out, allowing us to breathe just a little bit easier. Everything should be clear and unambiguous. There must be no loose ends. All issues should be resolved, and our hero and heroine should go off triumphant. They said he couldn't do it, but he did it.

These are the endings that we love. Harry marries Sally. King George VI makes a magnificent speech bolstering the morale of the British in the face of the German threat. These are clean, affirmative endings, satisfying our need for closure and "happy ever after."

Yes, you can give us a tragic ending, but do that and you risk losing your audience. In Peter Viertel's novel *White Hunter, Black Heart* (based on director John Huston's filming experiences in Africa), the young scriptwriter begs his director not to kill off his main characters. The words are from a novel but could have come from any book on scriptwriting.

> I'll say it in Hollywood terms . . . you've gone through hell with these two people. . . . You've improved their characters, made them see life with a humane, decent point of view, and then you kill them. And you kill them brutally, uselessly. I don't think an audience can stand that.

Well, all this theory is fine for the normal fiction film, but often *very difficult to put into practice in reality-based scripts.* Very many times *real life* has neither a conclusive ending nor a happy ending. Which can make a scriptwriter's task complicated, to say the least. Here, we are helped by the fact that in many cases the viewers already know the fate of the hero before they see the film. So they know that Amelia Earhart disappeared on a round-the-world flight, and that Christine, the heroine of *The Changeling*, never found her son.

Usually finding endings for murder stories is easy. In most murder docudramas, such as the stories of Amy Fisher and Carolyn Warmus, their trials give us a convenient climax. Yet what of more complex stories such as the *Exxon Valdez* oil disaster, or the Lockerbie Pan Am air disaster? It can be extremely difficult to find endings to stories like these. Often there is no obvious strong climax, no clear cutoff point, and no resolution of issues. What can you do in these cases?

Very often, you look for a link that will connect the beginning and the end that is not obvious from the story itself. In short, you look for bookends. This link can be a physical situation, an idea, or the words of a character. The point is that the link will clearly inspire thoughts of *before and after*, or *cause and effect*, or will sum up the film's message. This was the solution favored by Michael Baker in rounding off his film about the *Exxon Valdez* oil disaster.

> The end was a huge problem all the way through. There was no end in the sense the story just went on and on. . . . I eventually decided there had to be a very early cut off point and that would probably be within days of the spill. Also my main film characters had been called back or fired very early. So I was left without them for the ending.
>
> That was the "cut off." But there was also the question of shape. Once I knew the opening would be the beauty of the Alaska Sound, it was clear how the story would be enveloped. The pristine beautiful Sound at the beginning. The tarnished Sound at the end.
>
> The speech of President Bush that went over the ending was also

important. He says, "I am the environmental President," and originally I had put that at the beginning. But that gave the game away.
Putting it at the end sort of involves everybody. [The film] isn't just
the story of the Sound. It's about oil transportation, and that we are
all responsible to some extent.

166. End Sequence

*A dead and badly oiled bald eagle opens a montage of archive footage
depicting heavily oiled beaches, stagnant oiled pools, oiled birds; the visual
tally of the death and destruction wrought by the spill.*

NARRATOR (VOICE-OVER)

The commercial fishing season was closed down and the slick went on to
oil over 1,000 miles of Alaskan beaches. Upwards of over 400,000 birds
and many hundreds of mammals died in the spill, making it one of the
most lethal on record.

*After an interval, we hear the words of President Bush, addressing a
White House luncheon.*

BUSH (VOICE-OVER)

The Arctic National Wildlife Refuge in Alaska contains huge reserves of
oil and it would be irresponsible to ignore those. We have to transport
oil. We are becoming increasingly dependent on foreign oil and that is
not acceptable. . . . What you do is express the genuine concern you feel
on the environment and I do feel a concern, but not take irresponsible
action to guard against an incident of this nature. . . .

Where it is impossible to find this wrap-up link, and there is no easy
ending, you have to ask yourself, "What more would the viewer really like
to know?" This really amounts to:

What were the immediate and long-term results of the main events of the film?
What happened to the characters whose lives we have been following?

Answering these questions, my film on Ikey Solomon ends as follows:

NARRATOR (VOICE-OVER PICTURE)

In 1840 Ann and Ikey received conditional pardons. A few years later Ann
married Godfrey Levy and lived to the age of 92. Ikey died in Hobart in
September 1850, aged 65. His family went on to prosper in Australia, his
son becoming a noted businessman in Sydney.

During his lifetime Dickens neither confirmed nor denied that the character of Fagin was based on or inspired by Ikey Solomon.

Between 1804 and 1853, 76,000 convicts were transported to Tasmania. They had left one world in grief . . . little knowing that a new one, with immense hope and promise would open up, if not for them, then for the generations that came after.

Here, I put in the last sentence because I wanted the film to end on a slightly positive note after watching the painful trials of Ikey.

Paul Monash uses a similar technique to wrap up his film on Stalin. After passion and fury throughout the film, it all ends rather weakly. Instead of being assassinated, which would have given us a nice Julius Caesar scene, Stalin falls ill and dies quietly, surrounded by his ministers. To make up for the letdown, Monash then gives us an "update."

> *Three months after Stalin's death Lavrenti Beria was executed by his former associates.*
> *Three years later Nikita Khruschev began to reveal the nature and extent of Stalin's crimes, which caused the death of 40 million Soviet citizens.*
> *Nine years later Vasily Stalin died of acute alcoholism.*
> *Svetlana Alliluyeva now lives in England.*

Endings are difficult, but you try as best as you can. And if you can't think of anything, you tell your producer to make a film on Hitler instead of Stalin. He and Eva commit suicide. Their bodies are burnt. The allies advance. Their tanks are all over Berlin. The Reichstag is in flames. The sky is blood red. Now that's an ending a writer could really go to town on!

ADDITIONAL DRAMATIC DEVICES

A lot of people write good beginnings and endings but face difficulties making the middle of the script really work. Act 2 tends to be a long act, and unless you're careful, this is where the story can begin to drag. At that point, fiction writers occasionally use one or two dramatic stratagems to help speed things along.

The most commonly used device is the *reversal*. The hero's plan has collapsed, a simple solution seems out of the question, the villain has gained the upper hand, and the hero is left to face the enemy alone. The reversal helps the hero assess the situation totally differently and causes him to move in a new direction. In *The Changeling*, the discovery of the Wineville killings, and the possible murder of her son, secures Christine's release.

Reversals are very close to *surprise*, but whereas the former is usually negative a surprise can be negative or positive. The surprise is when the hero wins a million dollars, and when the most beautiful woman in town turns out to be his long-lost cousin. Both reversals and surprises are action points that can help you when you are in difficulties.

Another helpful device is raising the ante, or increasing the stakes, for both your hero and villain. This is the point of the film when you reveal that you are not talking of the loss of a few barrels of oil, and the ruin of a few beaches, but rather the loss of ten million barrels and a major catastrophe for a large part of the natural surroundings. This is also the point when you realize that the water will submerge the trapped miners in hours rather than days.

Your task in docudrama is to see whether your true-life story offers possibilities for use of these stratagems. In many stories, like the *Exxon Valdez* case, and the Baby Jessica situation, the opportunities for raising the ante are inherent in the original material. If so, think of using them. If they are not there, then be careful, because if the gimmicks seem too contrived or artificial, the audience will reject them out of hand.

In conclusion, let me repeat the main message of this chapter. You can write wonderful dialogue. You can bring your characters to life in a very convincing way. You can be faithful to all the historical aspects of your story. All these things are vital. But above all, you must get your shape and approach right. You must have a total overall vision of your film. Once you get that right, all the rest falls in place very easily.

SCRIPT EXAMPLE

Earlier in this chapter, we looked at some experiments in form. On this score, it's worth looking at Thames TV's *Letters of a Bomber Pilot*. The script was written by David Hodgson and is an excellent docudrama from England. What is of prime interest here is the way Hodgson combines reenacted scenes with straight documentary techniques such as the use of interviews and archive photos.

In *Bomber Pilot*, the scriptwriter's eldest brother, Bob, was a pilot in Britain's Royal Air Force and was shot down over Europe in March 1943. On his mother's death, David found a bunch of his brother's letters at the bottom of her wardrobe. All were written between 1940 and 1943 and describe the experiences of a young airman during the early years of the war. Written with humor and honesty, they described the training, the friends, the drinking, the crashes, and falling in love.

Using the letters as the basis of his script, Hodgson started by tracking what happened to many of the people mentioned in the letters.

It's a brilliant film, but its method is simple. Narrated by Hodgson, the film is grounded in a personal point of view. The letters, which form the basis of the script, are sometimes illustrated by library footage, and sometimes by reenacted scenes. Thus, occasionally an incident or a mood suggested by a letter will be fleshed out in a short dramatized scene. What gives the film its poignancy is that a number of people mentioned in the letters are tracked down and interviewed by the scriptwriter. So a friend appears in an on-screen interview, which then dissolves into a reenacted scene with actors.

The techniques are simple but work very well, as can be seen below.

Visual	Audio
Stills of Hugh Feast. Stills of Bob, Alf, and Hugh.	NARRATOR: Hugh Feast became one of Bob's closest friends. Like Bob, he came from London, and was just the same age. Just twenty. In November they were posted to RAF Shawbury to learn advanced night flying.
Archive footage of WAAFS (Women's Auxiliary Air Force). Hugh shuts door and walks to the bathroom watched by his friends, Derek, Alf, Bob, and Bob Wells.	Most RAF stations employed WAAFS in ground jobs, and not surprisingly romances blossomed. Hughie Feast was the first to be bowled over. Something that amused his friends. BOB: Now what's Mr. Feast getting dolled up for? ALF: He's meeting his WAAF. BOB: Again? BOB WELLS: This is the third time this week. It's serious stuff, isn't it? Let's lock his door.
Close-up of hands locking bathroom door. Medium shot of Hughie shaving. Bob peers at him from door. Lads run into dorm, followed by Bob.	BOB: (VOICE-OVER): Dear Joan, Hughie is going out with a girl from sick quarters. I believe he's taking her seriously.

What we see here is a fusion of three techniques: (a) voice-over archive footage and stills, (b) a dramatized scene, and (c) a letter voiced-over a dramatized scene.

As the film proceeds, various people are interviewed about their memories of Bob, and how they met him. The speech of his girlfriend, Bea Cauldrey, demonstrates how such interviews are integrated into the film.

Visual	Audio
Still of Bea.	NARRATOR: At the beginning of September, Bob came on a 48-hour pass, and went to a local dance. There he met a girl called Bea Cauldrey.
Medium close-up of interview with Bea. Pan with dancing couple to see Bea (actress) talking. Bob and his brother and sister enter.	BEA: My friend Doris and I went to this dance held by the Home Guard. Not many people came to these dances because the hall wasn't terribly big. I remember sitting on the side and then I saw this very tall man coming through the door.

And so the film goes on until we find out that Bob is missing. The fusion of drama and documentary style works very well. Altogether, it is a beautiful, moving, and painful film, especially at the end when we realize that of the hundred or so pilots who started with Bob, only a handful survived the war.

PART THREE

FROM TREATMENT TO SCRIPT

7. THE OUTLINE TREATMENT

You don't have to do a treatment, but it helps, especially in fact-based films. The treatment is your first attempt to outline the drama. It will show you and your commissioning editor several things:

The flow and development of the story
Who your main characters are
The situations they get caught in
The actions they take and the results
The focus at the beginning and end
The main confrontations and resolutions
The main action points
The sense of the overall dramatic build up and pace

The treatment is usually written as a series of loosely sketched *sequences*. They can be numbered or not according to your fancy, and they indicate a location and the action of the characters. Occasionally, they may contain dialogue or scraps of dialogue. Otherwise, they may indicate what the characters are talking about.

The opening sequences of my treatment on the British explorer Edward Palmer go as follows:

1. Lawns of Cambridge University, 1865. Crowds of students and lec-
   turers in 19th-century Dress. The building of Kings College dominates the scene. Voice of PALMER. Inside the college PALMER thanks
   the audience for making his trip to the Holy and possible.
2. A desert oasis. Three British officers stretched out in the sun. An
   officer arrive son a camel and dismounts. He indicates there is no
   word from Palmer, and he may be lost.
3. Dining room in luxury house. Dinner is over. Men in evening suits.
   PALMER is standing, pointing to a map. He indicates that this is
   Sinai, an unknown desert. Here the Children of Israel wandered for
   forty years. "Gentlemen, with my time, and your money, I intend to
   bring God to the heathen, and make darkness visible."
4. British headquarters, Jerusalem. 1878. Officers hovering. They are
   looking with heads puzzled at sketchy outline Sinai maps. Silence.

An orderly enters and clears the cups. Major BAGLEY worries that the Turks may have Palmer, his life may be threatened, and the gold will be lost. Captain FRANKLIN suggests he's already dead, and that Palmer was mad ever to go into the desert. BAGLEY, decisively: "There will be hell to pay if the story gets out. Palmer must be found."

As you can see, the treatment is written very much in a shorthand form. It's not a literary document for publication. It's merely a device to help you and the producer see where you are going, and what you want to do. Put your sequences together and you have a *step outline*. This easy reference shows you exactly how your script is built, and how every sequence relates to the development of the action and mood. With the outline as your guide, you can see at a glance the *function* of each sequence, whether it is necessary, and whether it is in the right place.

To show you an example of this, I analyzed the TV docudrama *Her Final Fury: Betty Broderick, the Last Chapter*. The plot revolves around Betty's murder of her former husband and his new wife. It ends with a second trial, and a woman D.A. is shown as Betty's main opponent in the film.

Sequence	Function
1. Murder of husband	Introduces Betty and action
2. Betty phones parents	Shows her fragile emotional state
3. Police at murder scene	Murder now becomes public
4. Husband's brother phones police	Introduces Betty's first opponent
5. Betty tells of murder	Introduces Betty's family
6. Betty turns herself in	Law has taken over
7. D.A. goes to work	Introduces woman D.A., Betty's chief opponent
8. Betty in jail	Loneliness, depression
9. Husband's brother arrives	Introduces funeral element
10. Visit in murder house	Atmosphere
11. Funeral of husband and second wife	Sadness, loss in husband's family
12. Betty denied bail	This and following sequences show the ugly sides of B's character
13. Betty demands new lawyer	

So far, the sequences develop the plot and give us two clear sides. On the one hand, stands Betty, on the other side, her husband's family and the district attorney. As the sequences proceed, we gradually realize that the main battle is between Betty and the woman D.A. We also have a number of action sequences that contrast with quiet emotional sequences, and as the film proceeds, we will get more and more juxtapositions of fury and calm.

The step outline also gives us a good sense of where the turning points are placed. In *The Final Fury*, the turning point is at the end of Betty's first trial. The jury cannot reach a verdict, and Betty is triumphant. The D.A. refuses to accept defeat and by her actions sets the scene for a spectacular second trial.

Some writers swear blindly by the need for treatments. Others view them skeptically, like Stephen Davis, whom I spoke to about the making of a true-life espionage film, *Yuri Nosenko, KGB*.

> I regard treatments as a bit of a nuisance. If you write a three-page treatment you'll be asked why didn't you write a thirty-page treatment. Do that, and then your producers will ask you why you didn't reduce it to three. If you write a detailed plot scenario you'll be asked if you could write an impressionistic, subjective, creative document. And that's the way it goes.

> I regard treatments with absolute dread. I think they are designed to win a consensus of some sort, at which point the writer can go away and do the real writing.

Most producers do in fact ask for a treatment, and one can see why. Besides helping you clear and organize your own mind, the treatment helps the producer see exactly where you're going before you're committed to the final script.

THE PROBLEMS OF DOCUDRAMA

At first glance, writing a treatment for a docudrama seems fairly straightforward. You select your most interesting events and episodes then order them in the most dramatic and compelling way. And 80 percent of the time, you'll be following a linear chronological progression. Unfortunately, in docudrama, the problem can be far more complex. In many cases, you know what attracted you to a story: the sheer newsworthiness of the blowing up of Yankee Stadium, or the attempted assassination of the Pope; but apart from that, all is jumbled and confused. There are things you cannot see:

What the focus of the story is
Who your main characters are
What the conflicts are

And underlying everything is your central problem, that your hands are tied. You can't just invent. You can't neatly sort things out in the way a fiction writer can because you are dealing with *true* events, and *real* people. Given all that, the writing of the first treatment becomes a little more problematic. Here, it helps to clear the decks. How do you start?

My own method is to *list on a few sheets of paper*:

The factual progression of the story, with all key dates and times included (you should actually have done this during research)

A few notes on structure and form, and possible approaches

All the elements that have caught my eye in research: interesting incidents, fascinating characters, main problems, conflicts between people, and so on

You can see below that this is very much the method used by Michael Baker when he started thinking about the scripting of his *Exxon Valdez* oil disaster movie.

> I don't see how I could have done without a treatment on this film. I wasn't required to do one, but in fact I did several. The first treatment was just looking at the story as a whole. It was a very long thing in which I just picked out salient sequences and scenes for a possible drama. What would be the entertaining scenes? What would be the revelatory? What were the details that were funny, or gripping, or made you laugh or cry? In other words, I was trying to find what was generally dramatic about the story, without attempting t find the key that would take me from beginning to end.

The treatments that followed were largely a process of whittling down the length, and getting it into shape, and that's what I think a treatment is for, to find the shape so you can start writing.

FOCUSING THE STORY

After laying out your lists, you try to focus the story. This means knowing what your story is about and where you're going with it. In most character stories this is relatively easy, and you should be able to answer the question of story and focus in one or two sentences. For example:

Infamous: This is about Truman Capote's flamboyant life in New York, and his attempt to write *In Cold Blood* (a book about a murder) in a new nonfiction drama style.

The Flags of Our Fathers: The film follows the fortunes of the three men who planted the U.S. flag on Iwo Jima, and the consequences that the publicity had on their lives.

In personality-centered films like *The Iron Lady* or *My Week with Marilyn*, it's usually easy to find the story and focus. Where the going gets rough is in films dealing with *issues, disasters,* and *public events.* The story may have captured the headlines, but it can be murder trying to find what is the *best story* or *angle* for the film. The only way out in all these matters is to consider a number of possibilities, and then go for the most dramatic, interesting, and entertaining solution.

Let's look for example at the famous Lockerbie air disaster. In 1988, a Pan Am jumbo jet was blown up over Lockerbie, Scotland, with the loss of over two hundred lives. The killers were thought to be Syrians or Libyans. As a result of Libya's refusal to hand over suspects, sanctions were imposed on the country by the U.N. Millions were sought in compensation by the relatives of the victims.

Problem: what story would one pursue for television? One can see various possibilities:

The lives of five victims before the tragedy
The assassins, the plot, and the getaway
The town of Lockerbie, before and after the disaster
The relatives versus Pan Am

The eventual film that was made for HBO was called *The Tragedy of Flight 103.* When I spoke to Michael Eaton, the scriptwriter, he told me that at first he thought the film would be about the terrorist groups who made the bomb, and the police operation against various Palestinian groups in Germany.

As the research came in, he and his executive producer realized there was a second vital story, that of the increasing breakdown of Pan Am security. The film could then be shaped as two stories, which eventually met in the explosion and conflagration.

As Michael put it:

It then became a story about two institutions, an international airline corporation and an international terrorist organization.

And the way I wanted to tell the story was to look at those organizations from top to bottom; from the boardroom to the people who sit by the X-ray machine, and examine your luggage when you go to an airport for a flight; from the people who go round the world looking for sponsorship for acts of terror down to the soldiers who carry the bags with the bombs.

So the film would be a juxtaposition between the way these two organizations work.

The problem of finding the story, or the right story, also faced Michael Baker when he worked on the *Exxon Valdez* spill story. I asked Michael whether the two sponsors of the film, HBO and the BBC, laid down an approach for him.

Not really. I think all they knew was that this incident had made a big impact in the States and they somehow wanted to recreate the story. But they didn't know how. As I continued researching it became very apparent that the story we were going to do was not the environmental story, because I'd watched twenty documentaries on that and there was no point in doing it again. That's another important thing about docudrama. You should always go for an angle that couldn't be done any other way. Otherwise what is the point of doing it as drama?

Anyway, it soon became apparent to me that the real story we were looking was the *political story* behind the disaster. The backsliding. The cockups. The Government trying to renege on its responsibilities. In other words, a fairly explosive story in journalistic terms, but also one that would be very dramatic if you could carry it off.

In regard to what story to tell, it's interesting to look at the differences between *United 93* and *Flight 93*, the first a feature, the latter a film for A&E TV. Both tell the story of United 93, another plane taken over by terrorists on 9/11, but their emphases differ. While both tell the stories of the passengers, *United 93* goes into great detail regarding the actions of the U.S. Air Force. Basically, I see this as a mistake, as in the end the air force did little. *Flight 93*, however, concentrates on the reactions of the relatives on the ground and makes for a more moving film.

SHAPE AND FORM

Though you have many things on your mind when you start your treatment, the question of shape and form may be the least of your worries. This is because the answers to both tend to crystallize in your mind through the whole process of research. By the time you come to consider a treatment, you will almost certainly have committed yourself to a clear linear approach or possibly to a more fanciful and inventive approach.

The nature of the material may also have determined your approach at a very early stage. Thus, if you are doing what almost amounts to a hard news investigatory story, you will probably opt for the simple chronological unfolding of the story. I said "probably" because both *The Thin Blue Line* and *Who Bombed Birmingham?* show how effective an imaginative use of the form can be, even in a police story. In the British TV film *Who Bombed Birmingham?*, the beginning of the film is framed as a television documentary.

If you are doing a biography, then you may have to think of a few variations. In *Milk*, Harvey Milk puts his actions and thoughts on tape. In *The Iron Lady*, one of the gimmicks used is to have Thatcher continually talking to an apparition of her dead husband. In *The First Fagin*, I had Ikey

Solomon looking back on his past from a room in Hobart, while the story is told in flashbacks.

CHOOSING THE CHARACTERS

Drama demands conflict and heroes, strong characters whose actions push the story forward. In fiction, you can invent characters to suit your needs. In docudrama, you have to select your characters from real life, and sometimes your choices are extremely limited.

The commonest problem, usually in disaster movies, is that you know the rough story yet the central characters evade you. Ideally you want a "hero" who will carry the story in the direction of your choice. Yet very often that character just doesn't exist. Besides story, that was the second problem of the Lockerbie film for Michael Eaton.

> We simply didn't have a central protagonist. There were several people who potentially arose to play that role but *as real life doesn't follow the rules of drama* they soon found themselves out of the picture.
>
> There was a man called Fred Ford inside Pan Am who was put in charge of beefing up Pan Am's security. But you quickly realized that was a cosmetic exercise. In a fiction film he would be the perfect dramatic protagonist. He would be the man who would fight bureaucracy, fight the institution, sacrifice his home and career so that truth will out.
>
> What happened in reality is that the moment he started blowing the whistle on Pan Am's poor security he was given the boot. Fired! He would have been the perfect protagonist but he was kicked out at the end of Act One. At that point I went back and looked at all the material very thoroughly. *And this is where the idea of a treatment is so useful.* I looked at the material and it seemed to me the only way we could tell the story was to center it around two institutions, Pan Am and the terrorists, because there wasn't one character who stayed the whole course of the drama.

The need to find the central character who could carry the story was also one of the key problems for Michael Baker in the *Exxon Valdez* film.

> For a long time we were interested in a fisherman who we thought would be a focus of tension. There was also a guy called Kelly Weaverling, who almost single handed, launched a kind of wildlife rescue operation which ran into the most appalling bureaucratic obstructionism. So I began to wonder if maybe we could reduce our canvas and look at the film through a Kelly story. Or should we do the captain's story [who let the boat hit the ice]. . . .

And one by one these stories were jettisoned. Kelly's was too environmental. With the captain's story there wasn't a real thread all the way through. He got taken off the ship and was then out of the story till the trial.

When the search for the right "hero" still fails to turn up a plausible central character, he or she may have to be created out of the author's imagination. This was the ploy used by Ernest Kinoy when he wrote *Skokie.* In the film, the central character, played by Danny Kaye, is a fictitious Holocaust survivor who objects violently to the real-life incident of neo-Nazis parading through Skokie. The technique works well and gives us a sympathetic main character who represents in himself the thousands of objectors to the march. There is problem, though, in using this device. Creating fictitious characters, or blending two people into one, can blur the boundaries between fact and fiction and can raise questions of credibility relating to the rest of the film. When you do things this way, use caution.

Skokie also raises the question of the relationship between character and conflict. Do you look for the conflict in news or disaster docudramas and find the character to carry these things, or vice versa? Again, Michael Baker was very perceptive about this dilemma.

> The *Exxon Valdez* story followed conflicts. Looking at the facts you saw that everybody had been in conflict. What I was looking for was the *right* conflict, one which wasn't black and white.
>
> I was very concerned that we show a story in which human beings were presented with a crisis and we could see what happened to them. And most of the time they screwed up. Almost the bottom line of the *Exxon Valdez* story was "give human beings a crisis and they'll screw it up."
>
> For me the film was not so much a search for conflicts, but because the story was such a sprawling one, a search for characters who could carry the audience through from beginning to end. But it had to be the right spread of characters to give you enough of the whole story. You couldn't be playing around with a character who was really a side show to the main attraction.

The story of the *Exxon Valdez* is, finally, not about the crash, nor about environmental pollution as such, but about the appalling human failures to stop the spread of the oil in the first three days. The failures embrace the Exxon company, officials from the state of Alaska, environmental protection agencies, and the company responsible for the first limitation actions. No one comes off well.

In the end, Baker focused on the actions of two men, Frank Iarossi from Exxon, and Dan Lawn from the Alaska Department of Environmental Conservation. How did Baker see them?

> Not as heroes. I wanted them to be human beings you could sympathize with. People whom the audience would root for but who were also fallible, faced with a crisis. Why the choice of Dan and Frank? First, because they were on different sides, and presented the axis on which the story could hang. In fact they never even met, which presented its own problems. Secondly it struck me that while they were people with different problems and agendas, they had a lot of affinities. They were both isolated in their own camp and both basically trying to do a good job.

Eaton and Baker have both, in their different ways summed up what you should be looking for in your characters when you come to do your treatment. For your own purposes, it may be worth making a checklist of the essential points or questions, and then seeing which of your possible characters scores highest. Your list will probably look something like this:

> Can he act as axis for the story?
> Is he with the story from beginning to the end?
> Is he sympathetic?
> Is he at risk through the story developments?
> Does he take action, or just observe events?
> Does he change in any way, or do we get to know him in a more meaningful way as the story progresses?
> Do we need another main character to show an alternative view?

REVISING THE TREATMENT

The treatment is an argument for your approach to the material. As I've said, it lets you and the producer see very clearly where you want to go and how you intend to get there. It shows how you intend to solve the problems of story character and structure. It shows you your entry into the drama, the growing complications, and the climax and resolution. And it shows you all this without your yet being committed to the script.

Many treatments are written in the form I showed you in my Palmer example, but it doesn't necessarily have to be that way. Many writers jot their suggested sequences down on cards, pin them to a wall, and start playing around with the choices and the order. Both ways work, and it's up to you to chose the one which best suits your temperament. However, just remember few producers will want to come up to your apartment to see a wall outline. On the whole they prefer the written out treatment.

Treatments are not static. You will often write three or four until you are satisfied. The first treatment of the Lockerbie disaster centered on the story of the terrorists. Only in the second or third treatment did the emphasis of the story shift to Pan Am's security failures. *Death of a Princess* started out as a straight dramatization of the princess's story. After a few months, that approach was discarded by Antony Thomas in favor of a journalist's search for the truth *behind* the main story.

As you proceed from treatment to treatment, you keep playing around with scenes and characters, testing and retesting their necessity, their use and their correct placing. For example, I asked Michael Baker what scenes got dropped as he progressed with his *Exxon Valdez* film.

> The fishermen were the main element we juggled with for ages. And even at the end there were people who wanted more of them while I wanted less. There were also a lot of individual scenes that stayed in for a long time and then got dropped, like a meeting of a committee of the Valdez Council. And the sort of ironic reason we dropped it was that although it was real, it was incompatible with dramatic reality.
>
> What happened was that many people were beginning to get concerned about tanker safety. And that the Coast Guard weren't doing their job properly. And someone said at the meeting, "Gentlemen. It's not a question of *if* we have a major spill, but *when.*" Then a few hours later the Valdez ran on the rocks.
>
> Initially everybody thought, "Great! This is what happened on the same night." But if you think about it, had you kept the scene in we would totally have undermined what was to come. So it came out of the script.

If you are lucky, you and the producer will see eye to eye on how the film should go. You discuss your approach with the producer—your angle on the story and the selected characters—and he or she says, "Good. Go ahead and see what you come up with." Occasionally, though, it can be quite sticky. In *The First Fagin*, for example, I had two producers, one German, one Australian. The latter wanted a film that emphasized Ikey's possible connection with Dickens and Fagin. My German producer, however, as I mentioned earlier, thought his audience wouldn't get the connection and wanted to put the emphasis on crime and punishment in England, and on life in the Australian penal colonies. Eventually, we compromised, but it wasn't easy.

Writer Stephen Davis also had this problem when writing a script for English television about a KGB spy.

> In *Nosenko* my problems were more with the producers than my own problem, how to make the script work. There were battles over accessibility and audience understanding. I think western audiences

are very sophisticated. They understand images and digest things quickly. Well, my American producers were firmly of another opinion. They wanted things to be slow, clear, and almost pedestrian less the audience fail to understand what was happening.

There were battles over the complexity of the intelligence case, and the number of characters. And there was a demand to simplify the narrative line. For example, the film seems to show that Nosenko was taken immediately by the British to a secure facility, when in fact he was held for a long time in an ordinary house.

DOCUDRAMA VERSUS FICTION

When you write, keep in mind there is one crucial difference between writing fiction and writing fact-based drama. One of the key attractions of fiction films is that usually the viewer *doesn't know the end of the story.* He does not know who killed Joe Smith. He does not know whether Harry or Bob gets Carol. He does not know which candidate will become president. He waits for the denouement and smiles in satisfaction when he finds out that Henry is the killer, or that Carol really loves Michael.

There is immense pleasure in the final discovery of plot solutions. Many ads warn us not to give away the end. Again, you would be furious at a friend who told you who the murderer was in Hitchcock's *Psycho.*

Reality-based films usually lack this basic appeal. Unfortunately, *we already know the endings.* We know the *Exxon Valdez* crashed. We know that Diana left Charles. We know that Margaret Thatcher became ill as she aged. So the films have to give us something else.

That usually amounts to a deep intensive exploration to discover several things:

Why something happened
How something happened
How the character behaved

The first two elements satisfy our curiosity to get to the heart of things, to go through closed doors and see how things really operate, to investigate the secret workings of organizations, governments, and bureaucracies, to gain access to the forbidden, to overhear, and to spy in silence.

An exploration of character allows us what we've always desired: to get inside someone's head, to look at emotions and actions that are often alien to us. It helps us explore thoughts and passions that are so different from ours, as Michael Eaton did in his film *Dr. Death,* about a doctor who murdered fifteen of his patients.

Obviously, these elements also appear in fiction films, but in docudrama they provide you with your basic approach to the script, as opposed to being peripheral considerations. It all seems simple, but you neglect this at your peril.

OVERALL VIEW

One of the mistakes you can make with a treatment is to work too hard on it, and to be too methodical and mechanical. You may know all about story rules, conflict, character choice, and focus, but there has to be a time when you let go. You can't write by numbers and according to formulae. As author Dwight Swain put it in a very good book on scriptwriting:

> The less attention you pay to mechanics when you sit down to do your first treatment, the better. Write from the moment's impulse. Get down everything in the wildest rush of enthusiasm you can muster. Hunt for the aspects that intrigue you, excite you, turn you on.

In other words, absorb the rules and hints, but then take chances, let go and jump in. Have fun. Later you can use all your rules as checks. They'll show you where your weak points are in structure or development, but the checks come after creativity, not before.

TREATMENT EXAMPLES

Throughout this chapter we've heard a great deal about the problems involved in writing the first treatments of *The Tragedy of Flight 103: The Inside Story*, and *Dead Ahead: The Exxon Valdez Disaster*. To finish off it may help to see what their partial outlines really looked like and then compare them to the final shooting scripts. I am also adding part of the treatment for *The First Fagin* that as accepted by my commissioning editor for ZDF in Germany.

The Tragedy of Flight 103: The Inside Story

The Tragedy of Flight 103: First Treatment. Writer: Michael Eaton.

1: Planes land at Frankfurt International Airport, one of the major crossroads of Europe. People from all over the world stand in line at the arrivals area. Among them MARLAN KHREESAT, a well dressed businessman from the Middle East waits at the customs checkpoint with his WIFE hovering behind him. The stone-faced CUSTOMS OFFICIAL is checking their Jordanian passports, and Khreesat tells him they've just come from Amman and he is on a working holiday. The customs officer tells him he has no visa to work in Germany and K. explains that he is on holiday to visit friends but while he is here he intends to renew contact with German firms which have supplied him in the past-he's an electrician. The line builds behind him, but the official slowly keys his name into a computer and consults a list of passport numbers. Eventually he asks how long they intend to stay and is told two or three weeks. The official finally stamps the passports and waves them through.

2: In the airport lunge a man sits waiting for them, reading a newspaper in Arabic: ABDEL GHADANFAR. He waves as they come through, wishing them "salam aleikum," but no names are used. He takes one of their bags and leads them out to the car park.

As they drive into Frankfurt, with passenger flights passing low over their heads, G tells Khreesat that there have been some interesting developments. New contacts have been made which will aid God's work on earth. K doesn't want to know. He has a specific task to perform, that's all. He wants to know when they will meet with their friend. K is told he is coming down from Neuss tomorrow, and K will return with him. Arrangements have been taken care for his wife to return with him next week. Her work is over, she's provided cover for the entry into Germany.

3: In Neuss, HAFEZ KASSAN DALKOMONI comes out of the Morgenland store, which is run by his brother-in-law ABASSI and meets with another PALESTINIAN outside. The man shows him a green Ford Taurus with Achen number plates. D. looks it over, takes the keys from the man, gets inside and drives off. These actions are being interrupted by a device (such as image freezing into a black and white photograph) to show that he is being watched or followed. Over this is the voice of a BFV officer briefing an operational unit. He gives a list of aliases for the man and details of his occupation and age (mid forties), address, and period of residency in West Germany. He is clearly pleased with himself as he announces that the surveillance photographs have been circulated throughout the security community and Israeli intelligence (the Mossad) has supplied a positive identification. He is Dalkomon-the finance officer for the Popular Front for the Liberation of Palestine-General Command. Part of his background involves serving more than ten years in Israeli prisons.

The treatment looks straightforward, but a number of things are worth noting:

Approach. In this first draft, Eaton centers his story on the terrorist group who made the bomb. This approach will change radically as more is found out about Pan Am's security failures.

Background and atmosphere. These two things are very clearly sketched in. For example, we can almost hear and see the planes taking off and landing when the Arabs exit the airport.

Details. Although it's only a brief outline, all necessary details are already laid down. A man is not just waiting in a Ford, he's waiting in a green Taurus.

Again, we are given an exact listing of all the aliases of the suspect and his exact address. (Note the importance of accuracy in these investigative-type docudramas.)

Action and development. While the first sequence is very innocent, the second hints at a mystery. By the third sequence, we see that something very fishy indeed is taking place and begin to place everything in a terrorist framework.

Treatment to script. What can be seen immediately is how easily the treatment can be turned into a script.

In the end, Eaton decided to start his actual script in a totally different way.

The Tragedy of Flight 103: Actual Script

1: INT. Lavatory stall. European airport
The locks of a battered suitcase are snapped open. The suitcase is opened to reveal the contents. Hands fumble with a small radio. A clock is attached to the radio with red tape and the radio is wrapped in a pair of pajamas. The suitcase is closed and a JFK label is attached to the handle.

2: INT. Gents lavatory. Day
A well-dressed man of Middle Eastern appearance comes out of the cubicle with a suitcase. He walks to the washbasin, looks in the mirror, turns on the tap. He is Vossi Langotsky.
CUT TO:

3: INT. European airport concourse. Day
LANGOTSKY *walks across the concourse carrying the suitcase. He reaches the Pan Am check in area and breaks into a run. He makes for a closed position where a porter is standing behind a desk.*

LANGOTSKY
Excuse me, could you get my case onto the New York flight?

PORTER
Baggage is closed now.

LANGOTSKY
Please, I have to be on that flight.

PORTER
They're already boarding.

LANGOTSKY
Well, I can't take it on as cabin luggage.
(The porter shrugs; Langotsky takes out a ten-dollar bill)
Listen, there must be some way to help. I have a very important engagement in New York.
He passes the ten dollar bill under the counter to the porter.

PORTER
I'll see what I can do.

Thank you.

The porter takes the suitcase. Langotsky laughs to himself at the ease of the operation and walks off from the check-desk.

Later, Langotsky watches the luggage being loaded on to the plane and calls the chairman of Pan Am. When he gets through he informs the incredulous chairman that he's just put a bomb on the plane. As the scene proceeds, we realize the bomb is a dummy, and that Langotsky is an Israeli agent employed to test Pan Am's security, which is obviously very bad. What astonishes us is that instead of applauding, Pan Am condemns the test as a stunt. And so we are into the film.

It's a fast exciting opening. It also tells us immediately what the film is about: not just the failure of Pan Am's security, but also the airline's refusal to take the subject seriously. The final script is very different from the treatment (partially due to ongoing research changing many perspectives, even as the script was being written) and it is fascinating to see how the two stories of Pan Am and the terrorists eventually weave together.

Dead Ahead: The Exxon Valdez Disaster

Michael Baker's research for *Exxon Valdez* took months. Below I've set out two extracts from his second treatment, one from the start of the film, one slightly later. Both extracts go into tremendous detail, making the end scripting that much easier.

Exxon Valdez Treatment: Writer, Michael Baker.

1: THURSDAY, MARCH 23, 1989: 8:20 P.M.

Panoramic view of Port Valdez bay ringed by a wall of spectacular snowy mountains that loom magnificently out of the darkness. Tint pinpricks of light are moving in the bay road. A taxi cab stops at the main gates of a brightly lit installation, the Alyeska Marine Terminal. Three men get out and are checked through a security gate. One of them is bearded Captain JOSEPH HAZELWOOD. Rising away from the car (crane shot) we have a view to the tanker berth loading cargo. Its name is clearly visible on the bow: EXXON VALDEZ. Panning off the tanker and across the water we pick out the lights of Valdez on the other side of the bay.

Probably the most dramatic scene in the film is going to be the crash itself. Baker understands that the viewer will want to know in detail how it happened. With this in mind, he lays everything out very fully in sequence fifteen of the treatment. The final script follows the treatment in almost every detail, with very little expansion in either action or dialogue.

[Treatment, continued]

14: the Exxon Valdez ploughs remorselessly through the darkness.

15: On the bridge we see the vessel is increasing speed up to 13 knots. Helmsman CLAAR is relieved by KAGAN. Just before leaving CLAAR tells COUSINS (the only officer present) that the steering is on automatic. COUSINS is surprised and instructs the gyro to be disengaged.

[From here on the sequence on board continues uninterrupted up to its fateful climax, as follows:]

The fathometer trace records a depth of less than 100 fathoms.

On the starboard bridge wing AB MAUREEN JONES is on the lookout. She sees a red light off the starboard bow flashing every five seconds. She enters the pilot house and warns COUSINS of this. He calmly acknowledges and continues to plot his fix on the navigation chart. Then he stares down at the radar scope looking for ice. AB JONES re-enters to report that the red light is now flashing every 4 seconds. Cousins again calmly acknowledges, then orders KAGAN to steer right 10 degrees.

After again checking the radar scope, COUSINS phones down to HAZELWOOD to report that he's started to turn back into the shipping lanes, adding, " I think there's a chance we may get into the edge of this ice." HAZELWOOD says, "Okay" and asks if COUSINS feels comfortable. "You know what you have to do?" COUSINS assures him he does.

[The depth of water decreases. The warnings flash. Apprehension mounts.]

The Fathometer shows the vessel in 30 fathoms.

Perspiring heavily COUSINS stares at the radar, then phones down to HAZELWOOD: "I think we are in serious trouble, sir. We have some kind of problem with the navigation . . ." A series of scraping jolts interrupts him, and he orders KAGAN to apply hard left rudder. KAGAN hesitates and COUSINS grabs the wheel, and frantically spins it hard left. The vessel starts to grind and clang as it runs aground.

HAZELWOOD races onto the bridge, and orders a hard left, then a hard right.

The Fathometer registers 0.

Down in the cargo control room First Mate KUNKEL stare sin horror at the holding tank gauges. He grabs the phone and tells HAZELWOOD that all starboard and center tanks are rapidly discharging. . . . On the bridge HAZELWOOD grimly puts down the phone and murmurs, "I guess this is one way to end your career."

One fairly late decision of Baker's was to "envelope" the story, to start off with a pristine view of the sound at the beginning of the film, and to show it's pollution at the end. Thus the film starts off in the day rather than at night. Apart from that, the script sticks very closely to the second treatment.

The First Fagin

My first treatment for my Ikey Solomon film went under a different name, *To the Penal Colony*. This was because my German commissioning editor wanted the film's emphasis to be on crime and punishment in the nineteenth century, rather than on the Fagin/Dickens connection. He'd read and liked my proposal but told me a four- or five-page treatment had to be submitted to his ZDF colleagues in Strasbourg, where it would be in competition with forty or so other proposals for the little money that was available. Below is part of the treatment I prepared for the Board.

The First Fagin: Writer, Alan Rosenthal

May 1827. Newgate prison, London. Two jail warders drag a convict through dark prison corridors, unlock a massive iron prison gate, and bundle their prisoner IKEY SOLOMON out into a foggy street. They push him into a hackney cab. As the cab proceeds through the misty streets, inside the warders seem to be drugged. IKEY bangs on the cab roof. The driver stops, unlocks IKEY, and gives him a hat and scarf. IKEY races off down the street.

The escape astounds London as IKEY, probably London's most famous criminal, was about to stand trial, and possible death by hanging. Wanted notices are nailed to trees. Pamphlets attributing the most amazing adventures to IKEY are sold on the streets. Two men in a pub discuss how Ikey trained boys to steal and shared a mistress with the Prince. A young Dickens note sit all down. So who was the real IKEY?

Title appears: TO THE PENAL COLONY (later changed to THE FIRST FAGIN).

1950: Van Diemen's Land, Southern Australia. Lashes of rain outside. Dark menacing trees. In a small room IKEY prepares to tell the viewers *the REAL story of his life*. He says people think they know about his life . . . because they see him as Dickens' model for Fagin in *Oliver Twist*. But it's all untrue . . . filthy lies. Now he wants to tell you the real story. As the film proceeds we return to this room again and again as IKEY supplements and comments on the story we see unfold on the screen.

Dissolve to LONDON late 1700s. Against landscapes of England and pictures of London, washerwomen, and markets etc., we get a picture of troubled times, and IKEY's Jewish background growing up in London's East End. A young IKEY, the pick pocket, is stealing from market barrows and eating fruit.

An older IKEY meets ANN. They fall deeply in love. After courting scenes in Ann's shop and home, they marry. The Jewish wedding under a

100 FROM TREATMENT TO SCRIPT

canopy. The Rabbi, guests, dancing and musicians are all shown in detail. But IKEY needs a job. He goes back to pick pocketing, which he did as a kid. When he attempts a theft at a public meeting, IKEY is caught red handed by the police. He is sentenced to the HULKS.

An historian, filmed against the river Thames, explains the nature of the Hulks. They were old warships which served as floating prisons for England's surplus prison population. Both the exterior and interior of the Hulks are shown in pictures. IKEY's life on the Hulks is shown in detail in studio reconstruction. He washes. Eats. Gets given clothes. Meets shipmates. One sees his daily routine as he works on the roads and in various harbors.

Rain. Autumn. Snow. Sun. The seasons pass. They are seen in all their moods. Then narrator tells us IKEY is released in error, but then pardoned.

Ikey's Return and New Life

A tired IKEY walks along a cobbled road. There is a warm passionate reunion with his wife. A historian on location in old London describes the changing world of England . . . political unrest, a land of the very rich and the very poor, with crime n the increase. Pictures and drawings are seen of London at that time.

In his Hobart room, talking to the camera and reminiscing, IKEY tells the viewers he wanted to change. See his family grow. He couldn't go back to pick pocketing, that would mean the rope.

Friday evening (Sabbath) at IKEY's house. It's shabby but comfortable. Candles are on the table. IKEY blesses his sons. Embraces ANN. The family is complete.

In Hobart room IKEY tells how he decided to become a businessman and start a new life.

London was an area of opportunity. Contemporary pictures of thieves' dens, prostitutes, crime areas, burglary. Petty thieving and burglaries are acted out. Crime is rife. IKEY describe show every area has its specialists. And IKEY becomes a fence, a receiver of stolen goods, the best in London. Trusted by all, and a standard price for all his purchases. How did he work? He takes instruments from a secret cupboard. He melts down silver. Examines silver marks. Examines forged bills. Tests the quality of linen. Examines some jewels very closely with a magnifying glass. Sorts out watches. Buys some small items from a thief. Cutlery and bundles are seen everywhere.

IKEY and his wife are seen in fashionable Hyde Park. IKEY is well dressed. His wife wears fine clothes. He is a success . . . a rich man. And his voice-over tells the audience this.

But in Hobart room, banging his pipe, IKEY tells how it all came crashing down.

IKEY's home at night. Police bang on the door and enter. They are looking for IKEY but only a frightened ANN is there. They cursorily search the living room, then force open the bedroom door. Watches and other stolen good are on the table. IKEY is now under threat.

Running feet down dark threatening streets. IKEY is on the run . . . for ten months. We are told he is caught. Police, looking for IKEY's other loot, search a warehouse full of clocks and linen. IKEY is charged with receiving stolen goods, and sent to Newgate prison to await trial.

Newgate Prison and After

An historian on camera in a prison outlines the history of Newgate, London's oldest prison. In IKEY's time it housed 400 prisoners of both sexes. We are inside Newgate. High grey prison walls. Contemporary drawings of Newgate prison and prisoners give way to reenactments. IKEY enters. Pays the guard. He looks around and sees drinking, prostitutes lying with prisoners, a few prisoners in chains. Others gambling and tattooing each other. We see a few cells.

The narrator outlines the barbaric penal code of the time, whereby 40 crimes merited the death sentence, and kids of ten could be hung. We see two cells set aside for condemned men, and IKEY relate show he watched a condemned man's last night.

As he does that we see a man carrying his coffin into chapel, and sit next to it as a chaplain gives a sermon. This dissolves into the condemned man mounting the gallows steps and getting hung.

ANN visits Newgate. The two plan an escape. IKEY is not going to wait for the noose. In a scene repeating the film's beginning IKEY gets into a cab with his warders. But the scene enlarges. The cab stops at a pub, and the warders are given drugged drinks. When the cab driven by IKEY's father in law MOSES resumes its journey, IKEY escapes.

As crowds in pubs read about the sensational escape, IKEY flees London by boat at night.

In his Hobart room IKEY tells how he fled to America. It was terrible to leave his family, but he faced hanging and he thought it would only be for a few months.

Humiliated, the police decide to take revenge by entrapping ANN. Back at IKEY's house someone plants stolen watches under the floorboards. Ann is being set up for theft by IKEY's brother. This is in agreement with the police, so that they'll free IKEY's father who is under arrest for theft.

Police burst into ANN's house. They do a brutal search and find ticking watches. In Court ANN is found guilty of theft and sentenced to 14 years transportation to Van Diemen's Land. She faints. In the same Court hearing IKEY's father is only given six months.

ANN is seen in Newgate prison writing a plea of mercy to the King. She is then seen in a ship's hold with her children. She is now a convict on her long voyage to Australia by sea.

And so the treatment goes on for another few pages, detailing Ikey's journey to Australia to find Ann, and his subsequent imprisonment there. The treatment was much shorter than those I usually write, but my brief was limited to five or six pages. Above all, I wanted to show two things very clearly. First, that the film would be a mixture of reconstructions and documentary scenes. I would like it to have been totally reconstructed, but knew our budget was insufficient for that. Second, I knew my German sponsors were very interested in showing the political mood of the times as well as Ikey's story, so that had to come up front as well.

On the whole, my final script followed the treatment fairly faithfully. Here and there, however, I added a few scenes that though not historically based added to the atmosphere. Thus, in the beginning of the film I had someone giving a reading of *Oliver Twist* in a pub, while Ikey looks on from the bar of the pub. When the reader of the *Oliver Twist* excerpts emphasizes that Fagin was a rascally Jew, and a receiver of stolen goods, a friend tells Ikey that could well be him. Ikey leaves the pub in disgust and then tells the viewers he hates that nonsense and wants to tell them his real story. In short, it was a further propellant into the film.

I also added a scene of Ikey singing in a pub in Hobart, after he has rejoined Ann in Van Diemen's Land. The function of the scene was to emphasize Ikey's happiness before the Governor of the island took aim at him. Was the treatment useful in writing the script? Very much so.

8. WRITING DIALOGUE AND NARRATION

On a recent journey, I read the following in an airline magazine. "Only rarely does Hollywood have anything interesting to say in terms of intelligent dialogue. Lines such as 'Hasta la vista! Baby!' and 'Go ahead, make my day,' now pass as the height of screen writing."

Well, it's a point of view, but not one I subscribe to. It misses the point. A writer doesn't set out to write the *best* dialogue or *intelligent* dialogue. He or she sets out to write dialogue most appropriate for the film.

Most stories today are either action driven or character driven, and there tends to be a different dialogue style for each.

Action films are mostly told with images and movement. We don't expect much baring of the inner soul of the hero. They are in life-and-death situations. The mere fact that the hero *can* talk surprises us. To expect him to say anything besides "damn" or "it's hellish cold" while sewing up his wounds, or clinging to an aircraft wing, would be over and above the call of duty.

Besides being brief, dialogue in fiction action films tends to be exaggerated, humorous, and unreal—but then so are the characters. We don't want a villain to speak like a Harvard professor. We don't expect him to say:

> Turner, my man, you've made a serious mistake. You could have stayed on the right side of the law, leading an honorable respectable life. But you agreed to join me in this venture. I don't think you have any option but to proceed along your chosen path.

What we do expect him to say is:

> You don't get it, Turner, do you? You've passed over now. We're partners in crime. There's no going back.

In these films we expect the dialogue to be brief, unsubtle, and to the point:

> You snitched. You're a stool pigeon. You've got it coming. So say goodbye to mama.

But what works for action-driven films doesn't work for character-driven stories. Here, the characters are trying to handle problems of love, divorce, guilt, passion, anxiety, financial and professional complications, and so on. Here we are dealing with a different kind of reality. The dialogue is going to be closer to real speech. It's going to reveal more of people's thought, their background, their hopes, their anxieties, their dreams. The dialogue is also going to be more subtle, more relaxed, more conversational.

This is not to say that the dialogue is not going to be funny, intelligent, and entertaining. *The Iron Lady* provides a good example here. Again, in *Barbarians at the Gate*, Ross Johnson, the CEO of tobacco company RJR Nabisco, can say of a new cigarette, "Tastes like shit, and smells like a fart. Looks like we got ourselves a real winner here. It's one goddam unique advertising slogan, I'll give you that."

In order to write dialogue for docudramas you have to have a feel for language and the nuances of speech. It's an art, not a technique. You can know all the rules, pay attention to all the hints and suggestions, and yet still be unable to write good dialogue. And you may know nothing, and yet have a wonderful facility for just getting dialogue right.

Now, after that warning, let me add that most of us *can* write fairly decent stuff, and that in a certain way it's easier writing film dialogue than conversations in novels. This is particularly true of fact-based dramas, where the dialogue tends to be very simple and straightforward, and is often based on diaries or reported conversations.

Before getting in deeper, let me suggest two things that will help you get into the right "mind frame."

First, before writing any dialogue, take a few minutes to really think about your characters and get inside their minds. Who are they? What motivates them? What type of people are they? Where do they come from? What makes them sad, happy, tense, joyous? These were the thoughts that guided me when I wrote the following opening speech for Ikey in *The First Fagin*.

IKEY

This vile portrait of the Jew Fagin, written by Charles Dickens. Now everybody thinks that Fagin is based on me and my past. All filth. A pack of vulgar lies.

They say my gang terrorized the city? My wife ran a brothel! I had a dozen mistresses! Well, ladies and gentlemen, welcome to the first installment of the epic story of Ikey Solomon, as told by the man himself. Do you really want to know what happened? Well do you?

Second, you should also ask yourself how much dialogue you really need. I know I've suggested that action films can get away with very little dialogue, but the same can often be true of character films. Even in character films, there are points where atmosphere and action speak louder than words.

For instance in Jane Campion's wonderful film *The Piano*, there are two key sequences totally carried by action. In the first, Ada's husband spies on his wife and finds her lying with Baines. A few minutes later, he grabs her, pulls her savagely through the woods, and tries to rape her. In a later sequence, the husband finds another proof of Ada's betrayal, seizes his axe and cuts off Ada's fingertip. Both scenes are played in virtual silence, the director knowing dialogue would have ruined the effect.

THE FUNCTION OF DIALOGUE

Dialogue has three essential uses:

To inform
To advance the plot
To reveal emotions and show the nature of the person talking

Most of the time, all three functions overlap, but it is essential that you, as a writer, understand the merits of each function by itself.

Giving Information

It seems very clear that you use dialogue to give information, so what's the catch? The problem is how to do that without your technique becoming too obvious.

Diana: Her True Story deals with the problems between Diana and Prince Charles. Here, it is vital for us to understand the ambivalence Charles has about marriage. But he is not an ordinary person. He cannot wait around indefinitely. He is heir to the throne, and marriage has consequences for the future of the monarchy and his relationship to the British people.

That's a lot of vital information, and writer Stephen Zito puts it all over in a conversation between Charles and his uncle, Lord Mountbatten.

LORD MOUNTBATTEN
Don't imagine that because you have become a sort of Royal pop idol that the British people will always support you. They'll back you only so long as they serve the country. And part of your duty is to marry and produce an heir. The people need to be assured the monarchy will continue.

CHARLES
It's true I don't want to get married at this time, but I recognize my obligations to the State. The trouble is there is no set role for me. I'm really rather an awkward problem.

LORD MOUNTBATTEN
It's only the monarchy that matters. For you and your wife, when you have one. So remember one thing, choose wisely.

CHARLES
You have my word, sir. (with a smile) I think I'd like to be King. I'm not so sure about being a husband.

Besides information, this dialogue also gives us a number of other things. It asserts, through Mountbatten, that only the monarchy matters. This is a vital point for setting up the film's conflict, because later Diana is going to assert that she, as a human being, matters, as well as the monarchy. Charles's last speech also sets the scene for the continuance of his affair with Camilla Bowles.

The style of the dialogue is also quite interesting. It shows Charles as a little bit stiff, formal, awkward. We begin to understand his character more deeply. Finally, the script makes a good point about scriptwriting in general: the frequent need for a good closing line. Here, we finish with, "I'd like to be King. I'm not so sure about being a husband." That line sums up Charles's approach, and we move easily into the next scene.

I've already mentioned *backstory*, and the need for information that precedes the start of the film. This is often given in dialogue between two characters. If done well, we should be unconscious that we are being fed information.

In the following scene, from the *Exxon Valdez* film, we are in the house of Frank Iarossi, one of the top executives of Exxon. Frank has just been told about the oil spill.

IAROSSI is speaking on the phone

IAROSSI

Until we know the scale of the problem, Craig just have everybody on alert. I'll get back to you as soon as I know more.
He dresses. His wife, in night gown helps him.

IAROSSI

I don't believe it. Twenty years without a major spill, and now we've got two in one month.

WIFE

Is it bad?

IAROSSI

I don't know. But that Hawaii spill we had three weeks ago was 35,000 gallons. That's big, and we cleaned up. No problem.

Baker's use of Iarossi's wife also reveals something else of importance in dialogue writing. In order to put information over via dialogue, whether backstory or current developments of the story, we normally need what I call the "bounce" person. Ostensibly, the speaker is telling the other person what has happened, or is about to happen, or how he feels, and so on. In reality, the author is often just using that other person as a bounce device to convey essential information to the audience.

A wonderful example of this is seen in the use of Margaret Thatcher's hallucination of her husband, Dennis, in *The Iron Lady*. Dennis is there to provide comic relief, but he also there for the audience to become privy to Margaret's private thoughts and hopes. So when Dennis proposes to Margaret, we also hear the following.

MARGARET
I love you so much . . . but I will never be one of those women, Dennis,
who stay silent and pretty on the arm of her husband. Or remote and
alone in kitchen, doing the washing up, for that matter.

DENNIS
We'll get help for that.
He leans forward to kiss again, but she pulls away.

MARGARET
No. One's life must matter, Dennis. Beyond the cooking, the cleaning, and
the children, one's life must mean more than that. I cannot die washing
up at any age.

DENNIS
That's why I want to marry you, my dear.

This bounce function is seen very clearly, also, in the script of *Barbarians at the Gates*. Here, it is clear that the wives of the central characters,
Ross Johnson and banker Henry Kravis, exist mainly to hear their partner's
troubles, and deflect this information toward the viewers.

Another way to reveal information is through commentary, which we'll
discuss later, is via the TV reporter. Most crisis stories sooner or later pull
in the media. It's therefore appropriate and handy to get some of your more
complex information over via the reporter. Thus, a real-life BBC reporter
keeps appearing throughout *The Iron Lady*. This strategy is also used a
couple of times in *Exxon Valdez* and works quite well:

REPORTER
According to experts this is by far the largest oil spill ever recorded in
U.S. waters. And yet apparently there are still well over 40 million gallons
of crude oil on board the tanker. . . . Deposit address Bank of America is
required to launch the emergency response . . .

As with anything else, you have to be careful of the reporter becoming a
cliché figure in these kinds of films. However, where the TV reporter is appropriate, use him or her to get information over that is just too difficult any other way.

Advancing the Plot

Your plot moves forward via physical actions but also via dialogue

POLICE CHIEF
Get that son of a bitch out of there, and see if we can use his room to make
an entry from the side. Is George here? He's necessary to cover our backs.

Probably a good deal of your dialogue will be written in this very direct
way. There is a problem and the character states very specifically how he is
going to solve it.

Revealing Emotions and Character

In films like *The Iron Lady*, *Stalin*, and *Diana: Her True Story*, one of our main questions is who is this in front of us? What are Maggie Thatcher's real dreams and ambitions? Who really is this monster who governs Russia? And how does Diana feel when she is up against the total power of the palace? In these cases, good dialogue is one of the best ways of revealing your characters, their feelings, and their inner turmoil.

In *Diana: Her True Story*, we follow the transformation of a rather innocent nineteen-year-old girl into a strong sophisticated woman. As she goes through crisis after crisis, her language becomes stronger, and her emotions are very powerfully revealed by everything she says. Good dialogue also reveals the difference in the characters and emotions of Charles and Diana, in a scene placed in their bedroom.

> DIANA
> I never get a kind word from you. A word of praise.

> CHARLES
> These things are to be earned.

> DIANA
> I'm trying so hard. All I need is a pat on the back now and then.

> CHARLES
> Doing well is what is expected.

> DIANA
> Then how about helping me to find my way

> CHARLES
> You have help. If you need something just ask Alfred or Christopher [courtier/advisers].

> DIANA
> I thought . . . after we were married . . . things would be different.

> CHARLES
> They are. You are the Princess of Wales. Royal duty is a wider and more permanent duty. . . . . There are things that are expected.

> DIANA
> But what about what the Princess expects?

> CHARLES
> You're not quite the girl of my engagement, Diana.

> DIANA
> Nor are you my Prince, sir.

In this scene the dialogue reveals Charles as a cold, unthinking prig. A call for sympathy, attention, love, and understanding is answered in the frostiest of terms. "Ask Alfred or Christopher." On Diana's side, we see something beyond the yearning and the desire for acceptance. We are beginning to notice the way she is maturing, and the strengthening of her backbone.

And with the comment, "Nor are you my Prince, sir," we once again have a sharp cut out of a scene.

In *Stalin* too, we see character revealed again and again by dialogue. In one of the best scenes, we find Stalin talking to Sergo. Stalin has suggested to Sergo that he return to Georgia and knock a few heads together.

STALIN

All you need are a good pair of boots. Feel this. (slapping boot) Go ahead. Feel it.

SERGO reaches down and feels the soft shiny leather

I could have been making these if my father had his way. . . . Wanted me to be a cobbler, like him. I ran away. Came home, he beat the shit out of me. But I never made boots for anyone. No, I wear them. And you want to know the best thing about them? (kicks out viciously) With boots, kick a man in the head and he'll never find his teeth. Wear boots Sergo.

He gives SERGO a playful kick in the ass.

Here we get two things. A bit of backstory about Stalin's origin, and a clear revelation of the man's viciousness and ugly sense of humor. The language is very vivid and graphic. "Came home, he beat the shit out of me," and "kick a man in the head and he'll never find his teeth." We don't need to know much more. The character of Stalin is set in these few brief words.

The power of dialogue also depends on what comes before. Take the words "I love you. I can't live without you." These are probably the most banal, overused phrases in film literature. But put them in a proper context, and they can be electrifying, as in Jane Campion's *The Piano*.

Essentially, it is a film of few words. The heroine can't even talk, and the hero Baines (Harvey Keitel), uses the shortest of phrases. Most of the scenes between them take place in the half-light, as Ada plays the piano and Baines gently caresses her. Finally, after Ada and Baines have lain together, Baines sits quietly in a chair and tells Ada not to come again.

BAINES

I love you, and I don't think about anything but you. But this is making you a whore and me miserable. Take your piano and go.

The point is Baines's words come from his soul and are so simple and true that we are almost moved to tears.

MAKING IT HANG TOGETHER

Your objective as a writer is to make the audience feel that the dialogue is natural, spontaneous. Sounds easy, and on the whole it is, providing you can see where the problems lie. What this amounts to is merely observing a few dos and don'ts.

Style

In all the extracts we've looked at, one thing has stood out. The dialogue has been appropriate for the person. At time, it's been a bit formal, but then Prince Charles is formal. At times, it's been a bit gross, but then Stalin was gross and boorish. At all times, the dialogue has been fairly close to our normal patterns of speech.

I say fairly close, because film dialogue is rarely just ordinary speech. It's often a bit heightened, a bit sharper, a bit pointed, a little bit more clever or incisive. If it weren't, it wouldn't work as well.

Dialogue style changes according to genre. In a detective drama, your dialogue will probably be hard and direct. Write a semicomedy, like *Barbarians at the Gate*, and your style may become more fanciful and exaggerated. Thus, what seems absolutely inappropriate for one script may be just right for another. Take for example some of the dialogue in the Australian series *Bodyline*.

The series deals with great cricket battles between England and Australia in the early 1930s. The English team seems to be using dangerous and questionable tactics, only just within the rules, and has injured an Australian player. The Australian underdogs are disgusted with their rivals and are close to quitting the series. The following dialogue then ensues on the train.

AUSTRALIAN CAPTAIN
He's got a cracked skull. There's no choice. We must quit.

FIRST AUSSIE TEAM MEMBER
There is, Bill. The same choice that all the battles have.

SECOND AUSSIE PLAYER
He's right. It's what built this country. Going out against all the odds and giving it your best. Our families came here as convicts. As settlers. They didn't shrink from the impossible. They went to places no one had ever been before. Then there were the shores of Gallipoli. Somewhere out there they taught us about courage. About loyalty to your mates, and about being Australian.

It's some speech, and all that seems missing is a reference to motherhood. In any other drama, it would have you rolling on the floor in laughter. Yet here it works beautifully. The style is absolutely appropriate for what is really a devastating war between nations, thinly disguised as a cricket match. Therefore, the references to honor, duty, and the past are emotionally correct and very appropriate for the script.

This slightly over-the-top style of dialogue is also used quite often in *The Iron Lady*. Margaret Thatcher is always used to giving speeches, so except when talking to her husband and her daughter, her dialogue sounds rather prime ministerish, and exhorting. And it works. Below, the U.S. secretary of state, General Haig, has asked Margaret to forget the Argentine invasion of the Falklands. It so petty, it doesn't matter. Margaret is triumphant in her scorn.

GENERAL HAIG

So you're proposing to go to war over these islands. They're thousands of miles away, a handful of citizens, potentially and economically insignificant, if you'll excuse me.

MARGARET

Just like Hawaii, I imagine.

HAIG

I'm sorry?

MARGARET

In 1941 Japan attacked Pearl Harbor. Did America go cap in hand and ask the Japanese for a peaceful negotiation of terms? Did she turn her back on her own citizens because they were thousands of miles from mainland United States? No, no, no! We will stand on principle, or we will not stand at all.

HAIG

But Margaret, we are used to war.

MARGARET

With all due respect, sir, I have done battle every single day of my life, and have been underestimated before. This lot seem bound to do the same, but they will rue the day.

Brevity

In general, we don't talk in long speeches, and when we're confronted with them, we tend to get bored to death, so where possible, keep your dialogue short. Not choppy, not brusque, but short. However, when you have really good dialogue, or a fascinating story, you have a chance to get away with anything. In *Death of a Princess*, Antony Thomas has an old princess relate the following to Ryder, the journalist who's seeking the background to the execution.

THE EMIRA

Sex. Maybe that's a privilege. To relieve their boredom, these princesses live the most interesting and busy sex lives. Very little romance. Quick liaisons. Sometimes cruel, always dangerous.

RYDER

How do they make contact with the men?

THE EMIRA

The chauffeur and personal maid. They make the contact and have the secrets. Of course they bribed, heavily bribed. The irony is that it's the woman who chooses the man. There are always ways of finding a man. The sword dances on national days. This is a great opportunity for men to show off. At night, in the desert. The women sitting in their cars, in the dark, watching men, selecting men. . . . There's a road in the desert. Women go there to look men over. Every evening at about five. . . . When they choose a man if it works, it works. And if it doesn't, they just move on. If they find a man attractive, they just write down his number and tell the chauffeur to make contact.

The speech is long, but what makes it work is that it is absolutely hypnotizing. The facts being revealed go against our normal concepts of the behavior of Muslim women. We want to know more. So we listen, entranced. I should add that the speech also shocked the Saudi Arabians and led to a temporary breech of diplomatic relations between them and the British.

Style, Grammar, and Colloquialisms

People don't talk like stuffed dummies or like the *Oxford English Dictionary*. They don't talk like grammar books, nor do they sound like the queen of England. They let their hair down when they talk, and they use slang and colloquialisms. So if a character sees a newspaper article with a harsh write-up on herself, she probably doesn't say, "What a stupid article." She'll say, "Get outta here."

We normally talk in very simple unaffected ways, and men and women also talk slightly differently. It's not just a matter of the subjects they talk about, but also the style in which they express themselves.

Occasionally, we also swear for emphasis, and what is permitted in scripts has varied over the years. Once, the Hollywood production code fined David Selznick $5,000 for having Rhett Butler say "I don't give a damn." And it was only a few years ago that the BBC executives nearly had heart failure when Kenneth Tynan said "fuck" on one of their programs. Now, it is a rare detective or action film that doesn't have swearing sprinkled liberally over the script. Even on TV, which is a little more prudish than mainstream cinema, "hell," "bullshit," and "who gives a crap?" are also used to add color. And no women's prison picture would be complete without expressions such as "shake your butt you sadass bitch."

In these films, the tone is right. It's tight. Combative. Compact. Confrontational. And slangy. But you have to be careful. Too often, swearing or loose language is just a substitute for thinking about your script. The only rule is to write what is appropriate for your character. The inmate can say, "I'll bust your fucking ass, you mother fuckin' son of a bitch," but that's not the language you'd use for the royal family. As the old saying has it, horses for courses.

Preaching

Another difficulty that confronts the docudrama writer is how to avoid being preachy and didactic. This is the trap that awaits you particularly in historic films and in issue-oriented films.

Hitler dies, and if we are not careful, we might have some colonel saying something unrealistic:

COLONEL

We let him get away too long. Humanity must now see that scum like this never rule the earth again. Finally we have reached the light. That light must never be extinguished.

We hear this and wince in pain. If anything works, it's dialogue that goes the other way. That's why the beginning of *Patton* is so refreshing. Patton stands in front of his troops, and, instead of exhorting them to a glorious death, says, "The good soldier doesn't die for his country. He makes the enemy die for his country."

However, as I pointed out earlier, you will occasionally go for over–the-top dialogue. *The Iron Lady* gave us one example, and Paul Monash's *Stalin* gives us quite a few examples that are even more preachy but that work. So when Lenin returns from exile, we are actually waiting for the following:

> LENIN
>
> Dear comrades, soldiers, sailors, workers. I thank you for overthrowing the Tsar! But the great world war continues. Did you overthrow the Tsar to continue his bloody war?

> CROWD
>
> (thundering) No!

> LENIN
>
> But it does continue! Did you overthrow the Tsar so the peasants would re-main landless . . . so the workers and their families would continue to starve?

> CROWD
>
> No!

> LENIN
>
> The people demand peace! Now! The people demand land! Now! For-ward to the international social revolution, the unfinished revolution, the proletarian revolution.

It's great stuff. We enjoy the speech in exactly the same way we enjoy Churchill's pugnacious war speeches: "We shall fight them on the beaches. We shall fight them on the land." These are words totally appropriate to the man, the place, and the time.

In most films, there also comes a time when you need to sum up the issues. This may happen in the middle of a film, or you may want to sum-marize at the end. This happens particularly in films on crisis situations, or national threats. The disasters on 9/11 have led to a new age in America. Hurricane Katrina has led to a revaluation of the safety of New Orleans and how it looks at the future. But we must use care in how we sum up. Michael Baker gets away with summary in the speech he gives to environmental officer Dan Lawn at the end of *Exxon Valdez*, but it's a close call.

> DAN
>
> Listen, I'm not against oil. I started as an engineer. Helped build the pipeline and was proud of it. But we all get hooked on that black stuff. Oil made the living easy. Now it's choking us to death. (Beat) But it needn't have happened. The state was warned and did nothing about it. Hell, this state has earned $30 billion off that pipeline. A lot less than one percent of that has ever gone to environmental protection.

Having Fun

But what if, in the end, in spite of knowing all the rules, and absorbing all the hints, your dialogue fails to breathe? This is usually because you have been working so much with your head, as opposed to intuitive feeling, because you've lost the spirit of the thing. So sometimes, it's useful to forget everything, take off, and have some fun with the script.

Some years ago, David Mamet wrote a short play that was turned into a film called *About Last Night*, with James Belushi. At the start of the film, Belushi's character tells his pal Rob about his experiences with "a great broad." The monologue lasts about seven minutes and is hilarious. "She gave me these eyes. What eyes. I got into bed. She stripped. The bed caught fire. I'm waiting. Can I finish before the fire engine comes?" In practical terms, all the script is doing is telling us that the guy Belushi is playing is putting it on, and Rob is less experienced. Yet to put it that way would be to miss the terrific fun we have hearing the story.

I've taken this example from a fiction film because this "loosening up" isn't seen very much in docudrama. It's there in *Barbarians at the Gate*, but otherwise it's a rare quality in fact-based films. It's a pity, because when you put logic aside, and take off with your imagination, you and the viewers can have a great deal of fun.

A wonderful example of this appears in David Seidler's Oscar-winning script for *The King's Speech*. Most of the comic sequences in the film derive from the wonderfully funny dialogue exchanges between the uptight Prince Albert (Bertie) and his unorthodox speech therapist, Lionel. The following altercation takes place when Bertie visits Lionel after a depressing confrontation with his elder brother.

LIONEL
You seldom stutter with me anymore.

BERTIE
Because you're paid to listen.

LIONEL
Like a rebel geisha girl?
    Both of them contemplate battered toys in LIONEL's study. The room is cluttered.

BERTIE
I couldn't say anything.

LIONEL
You could have refused. Do you know any rude words?

BERTIE
What a bloody stupid question. I just said one. Bloody. Bloody. Bloody.

LIONEL
Perhaps a touch more vulgar?

BERTIE
Certainly not!

LIONEL

To prove you know how.

BERTIE

Bugger.

LIONEL

A public school prig could do better.

BERTIE

Well bloody bugger to you, you beastly bastard.

LIONEL

Hardly robust.

BERTIE

Shit then. Shit. Shit. Shit.

LIONEL

See how defecation flows trippingly from your tongue. You don't stutter when you swear.

DOCUDRAMA DIALOGUE: SOURCES AND INSPIRATION

How does reality restrict your canvas? If this is the general question that confronts you the whole time when you write dramadocs, you face one of its most difficult aspects when you come to compose dialogue. You are dealing with real people, real lives. What liberties can you take with what they say? How much can you invent? How important is it for you to be accurate with the dialogue? Is it even possible? And what will be the effect of the things you say on film characters who are still alive?

The questions are endless. There are no easy answers, and in the end everyone has to carve out their own personal positions. The attitude you take should be a little bit practical, a little bit philosophical. When I was researching this book, half the writers I talked to said, "Accuracy. That's the only thing that counts." The other half discounted that as impossible. For example, I queried Peter Prince, the author of the Oppenheimer series, about his attitude to docudrama dialogue.

[In *Oppenheimer*] ninety percent of the time I had to invent the dialogue. . . . There were one or two memorable statements to play with, such as "I am become death, the destroyer of worlds," and there were the congressional hearings, but most of the dialogue was made up.

How does one deal with characters based on real live people? The short answer is I never considered the reality of the people behind my characters. This sounds arrogant, but I believe it takes a certain kind of arrogance to write any drama, and certainly to do the thing that is anathema to academic historians . . . to put words into the mouths of historic figures.

Before writing my script I interviewed many of the survivors of the Oppenheimer era. It was enormously helpful to me, both for what people told me, and for the impression they gave of themselves. But having extracted what I could from them, I felt I had to shield myself from their independent reality if I was going to work up the nerve to make these people "my" characters.

I understand Peter's point of view, but in *The First Fagin*, I worked in the exact opposite direction. I read all Ikey's letters, and there were many, and his speeches in his court appearances. I wanted to get the flavor of his speech and more importantly what he felt. Having begun to understand slightly how his mind worked, I tried to make his dialogue as authentic to the man as I could.

On a simple level the argument would seem to be: Are you a dramatist? If so, then all is possible. Or are you a journalist? In this case, you want to get as close to the truth as you can. In fact-based films, you want drama, and you want the truth. You want to have your cake and eat it, and at times the meal can be quite hard to digest.

Boundaries

If you write about living people, your dialogue and your portrayal of these characters need to take notice of the laws of libel and privacy. This is a hefty subject and may well affect what you say and how you say it. Rather than talk about it here, I've discussed the whole subject at length in chapter 13, which deals with many of the legal aspects of writing docudrama.

You may also run across the problem that your characters themselves want to tell their own story without your help. This happened when Granada TV and HBO made a film called *Hostages*, about the seizing of four British hostages in Lebanon. This is what the hostages themselves wrote when they were released, soon after the making of the film.

> We are all writing personal accounts of our experiences, and do not see how the co-producers can think they have the right to produce a story reporting to be true before those at the centre of it have come to terms with it themselves. Without our co-operation Granada have felt it permissible to invent very intimate aspects of our captivity and liberation. We feel that to do this while claiming the film is "true" is both highly insensitive to the hostages and their families and a serious abuse of public trust.

In spite of the criticism, the film was screened as planned.

Audience

To a large extent, the kind of dialogue you write is closely tied to the demands and expectations of the audience. Write a historic drama about Columbus, and no one will bother too much about what he says. Write a cozy comedy about songsmith George M. Cohan and call it *Yankee Doodle Dandy*, and again few people will question the dialogue. But write about the tragedy of 9/11, or the Iraqi war, or Hurricane Katrina, and people will expect the dialogue to be much closer to reality and the truth.

Why is that? Because in these cases, we really want to understand what happened, and how people really behaved in these crises. We turn to films like *United 93* or *And the Band Played On* because we want to get very close to the truth, and therefore accurate dialogue is of some importance to us.

Character Accuracy and Invented Dialogue

Having said all that, could it be that in aiming for accurate dialogue we are attempting mission: impossible? You weren't there when Hitler committed suicide, or when Caesar was assassinated, and even if you were, what you heard would probably be very undramatic. There's a lot of difference between saying, "This knife in my ribs hurts like hell," and "Et tu, Brute?" or between a passerby saying, "Cleopatra's a great-looking girl," and Enobarbus's comment, "Age cannot wither her, nor custom stale her infinite variety."

What one aims for is gripping dialogue that is appropriate for the time, the place, the character, and the situation. We really don't know what Charles and Diana said to each other in bed, but his remarking, "You are not the girl of my engagement," and her answering, "Neither are you my Prince," seems well within the realm of possibility. In *Hostages*, writer Bernard MacLaverty created imaginary dialogue exchanges between the prisoners in the Arab cells. While the overall scenes were based on fact, the specific dialogue came straight out of MacLaverty's head but nevertheless captured the idiom and spirit of the characters.

Recorded versus Nonrecorded Meetings

We live in an age of tape recorders, interview, memoirs, and court transcripts. How do you manage this material in terms of creating dialogue?

You select. You decide one scene is absolutely dependent on the original material, and another scene can use the materials in a more liberal way. What are your criteria? You do what works best in creating an absorbing drama that is still an accurate interpretation of the original events portrayed. This is the way Michael Baker tackles the problem:

> Let us say you have a record of a meeting, completely verbatim. In that case it's a question of selecting what are the best bits. Usually, what you are left with, after having talked to all sides, or as many sides as possible, is nothing like a verbatim report. What you get is a sense of the spirit of the meeting, and what people's positions were. And on that basis you reconstruct it in as dramatic a form as possible.

And nearly always... what amazes me about the difference between dramatic reality and reality (because of the inherent need for conflict in drama) is that these meetings as scripted are much more "keyed up" and angry than they were in real life. This was certainly true in the *Exxon Valdez* film. There the original meetings were very low key. The anger came afterwards.

Michael Eaton, the writer of the film about the Lockerbie air tragedy, puts the situation this way:

I'm a dramatist, and I write the dialogue on the basis of all the source material I have. I take the sources, I take the interviews, I take the journalistic information, I take the public record, and then I put words into people's mouths.

Now sometimes you are writing about a secret meeting, and that can be difficult. So what do you do? You know a meeting took place. A secret meeting between certain people. We know what positions they took at that meeting. So we know what the agenda of that meeting was and what arguments the participants would have used. We also know what actions arose from that meeting, what consequences flew out of it. Therefore, we are in a pretty good position to decide which perspective and point of view was in ascendancy. We know all this, and we go away and write. You might see this as an area or an attitude which is open to an enormous amount of criticism, but I don't see a problem with it really.

Later, I discussed with Michael the question of distortion and misrepresentation of people, and their views and actions. How does he deal with these things.

Throughout the whole process of composition I am in constant contact with the lawyers acting on behalf of the TV company making the film. I send them drafts. I send them scenes. And in those scenes I am giving my sources and informing them what lines of dialogue are actually taken as verbatim record, and which I am inventing on the basis of those sources. And the lawyers are informing me of what I can and can't do. And if there is a difference of opinion between the lawyers and the dramatist, I'm afraid it's the lawyer who wins. [There is a further discussion of this subject from the point of view of the TV company in appendix A.]

When you write reality-based films, you are often asking people to trust you. I'm not talking about those who've sold you their story for $100,000 and then keep warning you about libel actions. I'm thinking about ordinary people who think the story worth telling, and have put their faith in you to tell it accurately. So what do you do when you know that telling their story or using their words can endanger them. They've told you about their past in the Mafia. They've named names and keep looking over their shoulders in terror. What do you do in cases like these?

This situation happened to Antony Thomas while researching *Death of a Princess*. Thomas's solution seems a good way out of the difficulty.

> When I started re-contacting my interviewees and said, "I'm think-ing of doing a documentary and want you to repeat what you said to me," almost without exception they said, "Are you mad? We are never going to appear in a film making these statements about Arab society and womanhood and Saudi Arabia. It's impossible."
>
> So I moved to a second stage and said, "What if I dramatize this journey?" Then I questioned everyone I had interviewed and asked them whether, if I used their exact words without editorializing them or changing them, would they trust me to create a character who is completely from themselves, exists in a different context, yet speaks their exact words. The permissions were given and formed the basis for the film. I took the interviews, cut them down slightly, but was careful to maintain what remained word for word, as in the original.

In this case, Thomas's sense of faith to the original text was vital to the integrity of a picture that became mired in controversy. After it was screened, it caused a rupture in diplomatic relations between Britain and Saudi Arabia. A U.S. oil company even took out an ad in the *New York Times* accusing Thomas of inventing a fairy tale. The defense was that the stories and the dialogue were 100 percent true.

NARRATION

In recent years, there has been an increasing use of commentary or narration in dramadocs. It is easy to see why this should happen. Narration is often one of the simplest and most effective tools for solving a number of your film's difficulties.

Narration can quickly and easily set up the factual background of a film, providing simple or complex information that doesn't arise easily or naturally from the casual conversation of your characters. It can complement the mood of the film. It can provide focus and emphasis, and it should help the viewer to understand more fully what is on the screen. In a compact and elegant way, narration can help focus what the film is about and where it's going.

Often, the narration sets the scene for you and tells you what to expect. So the Canadian film *Democracy on Trial: The Morgentaler Affair* simply begins:

NARRATOR

It is the first of June, 1970.

What is about to happen here will be the beginning of the most contro-versial legal battle of the decade. A battle that will shake the Canadian justice system to its foundations.

The police, however, know nothing of all this. They are here for a routine raid on the clinic of an abortionist.

As this film about a crusading doctor proceeds, we follow Morgentaler through three complex court battles to keep his abortion clinic open and fight off jail for himself. Narration sets the scene and is also used frequently to cut away from the actors and comment on what is happening. The nar-ration is also used to bridge immense time gaps.

PRIEST

Our unwanted children will be joined by their unwanted elders. Euthana-sia will have as many headlines in a few years as abortion is getting now.

NARRATION

As the debate heats up anti-abortion groups start to apply political pres-sure, rallying thousands of supporters in front of the Parliament buildings in Ottawa. They find a sympathetic listener in Justice Minister Lang.

LANG

I disagree completely with the proposition that it's just the decision for the mother . . .

NARRATION

But despite the anti-abortion campaign, six months after the raid the clinic is still open for business. Several of the nurses are also facing crim-inal charges, but no one has any regrets.

Here, the narration is clearly identified as narration, but it can come dis-guised in many forms. In *Exxon Valdez*, as we pointed out, vital information is supplied to us by the TV commentator. The TV show is a nice gimmick, but the reality is we are using commentary, only slightly dressed up.

Another method for disguising commentary is to have it put over by one of the minor actors in the drama. In the Australian TV series *Bodyline*, the narrator's task is shouldered by the hero's girlfriend. She is the one who tells us what cricket is about, a thankless task given the complexity of the game.

Style and Language

The principles for writing narration are similar to those for writing dialogue.

Writing for the ear. The journalist writes for the eye, but in narration you write for the ear. This means you keep your vocabulary simple and easy to understand.

Grammar and Slang. Most of the time your writing will be relatively standard. You can be ungrammatical, and you can use slang, but you probably won't, for a good reason. Narration stands in contrast to dialogue, and you'll probably leave the looser language for the latter.

Simple, powerful sentences. Narration appears to work best using simple, strong sentences, with the main verb close to the beginning. Here's what I mean by a simple sentence. "The American troops were young and untried. They came from Texas, Utah, and Oregon. Few had ever been east. Now they found themselves 5,000 miles from home, ready to invade Europe. It was June 5th. Few knew it, but D-Day was only hours away."

Atmosphere. With narration you can also add an extra dimension to what you see on the screen. The jeeps don't just go round in the night taking men to planes. They go round "in the bitter cold, through clinging mists, carrying men to the dark outlines of the waiting planes."

Does narration really fit in with straight drama? I think so, and it's certainly been with us as far back as Shakespeare. After all, isn't Chorus in *Henry V* just our narrator in different garb. So play around with narration and see where it can help, not just to get you out of a tight corner, but also to add something different to your film.

9. Beginning Your Script

The moment has come when you are ready to start the script itself. Your first task is to make sure that when you do write, your work follows the standard conventions for script layout. They are fairly simple, and many of the rules you will have picked up by merely glancing at the script examples earlier in the book. You'll have noticed, for example, that each sequence describes setting, action, who is present, and the dialogue. All this now has to be examined in a little more detail.

THE SCRIPT FORMAT

Cast Lists

This is not absolutely necessary, but if you are writing a TV show with an immense cast of characters, it's useful to identify them at the beginning of the script. The introductory page to *Exxon Valdez* looks like this.

DEAD AHEAD: THE EXXON VALDEZ DISASTER

CORDOVA (The Fishermen)

Rick Steiner	Marine Biologist
Jack Lamb	Acting President, CDFU
David Grimes	Fisherman/poet/folksinger
Dr. Riki Ott	CDFU pollution specialist

EXXON

Frank Iarossi	President, Exxon Shipping Co.
Craig Rassinier	Exxon, oil spill response coordinator

STATE OF ALASKA

Dennis Kelso	Commissioner, ADEC
Dan Lawn	ADEC's local man in Valdez

The list then goes on, identifying people from the Coast Guard, from the crew of the tanker, from the pipeline company, and from the presidential delegation.

Explanatory Captions

Many fact-based TV dramas use short captions at the beginning of the film to explain the background of the story, their sources for the script, and (sometimes) how and where they have fictionalized. The caption for Granada TV's *Who Bombed Birmingham?* sets things out this way.

CAPTION

On the night of 21st November 1874, two Birmingham public houses were bombed by The Irish Republican Army. 21 people were killed and 162 injured.

Six men were convicted. They have been in prison since 1974. In 1985, three journalists from the TV current affairs program, *World in Action*, began examining the case. Drawing on court transcripts, taped interviews, and contemporary statements, this film is a three-year reconstruction of a three-year investigation into the true story behind the bombings.

Sometimes, captions are used in the body of the film to indicate uncertainty, and to show the audience what you, as a scriptwriter, are doing. What happened in the final hours leading to the Lockerbie air disaster is shrouded in mystery. This is covered in Michael Eaton's script as follows:

INT. MALTA AIRPORT. DAY
PAN DOWN TO PICK UP SALEEM WALKING TOWARDS THE AIRPORT ENTRANCE CARRYING THE SUITCASE.

NARRATION OR CAPTIONS OVER

The precise events of the day which was to end with the deaths of 270 people remain unclear and the subject of the biggest murder investigation in history. But official reports and records, supplemented by our own investigations point to a pattern of security failures which marked the day of the tragedy.

The Basic Format

For the most part, the layout formats or conventions for both film and TV scripts are virtually identical. There are slight variations in formats for tape scripts, but nothing worth bothering about.

Scene setting. The first thing the script has to indicate is location, time of the day, and whether the scene takes place indoors or out. This is done using upper case. The scene is also given a number. What results looks like this:

INT. BETTY'S HOUSE LA JOLLA. NIGHT
or

EXT. MALTA AIRPORT. DAY

As you can see, abbreviations are used for "interior" and "exterior."
Action and character description. Action and character description are set in lowercase and go the full width of the page. When character's names are mentioned, they are referred to in uppercase, as you can see below.

EXT. NEW YORK COUNTRYSIDE. DAY
  Early dawn on a lonely country road, a day full of promise. A ribbon of light on the horizon. The sound of birds. JOHN STONE, a handsome man in his late twenties, very middle class, is leaning against his Cadillac, reading. His chauffeur GEORGE, mid-forties, rumpled, has stripped off his shirt and is changing the car tire. A car with its headlights on enters the frame.

Here the action is clear, and we have given a minimum description of John and George. We could have elaborated and said John is a Harvard grad, and snobbish, but that will probably emerge later. In the above, we are really setting the scene. Later, we may want to describe real action.

  JOHN listens in disbelief. He strikes his head as if to hammer home the message. He is clowning. He draws a hand down over his face to wipe away the laughter. FRANK moves towards him and suddenly punches JOHN in the stomach.

In many British post-production scripts, such as the example from *Death of a Princess*, the action may be described in upper case. That's fine, except the characters don't stand out so clearly.
Dialogue. We center the name of the person speaking, and then print the dialogue in lower case, set in from the margins.

FRANK

I thought the big boys had taken care of that stool pigeon. You mean I'll have to waste another bullet on him? Well, maybe I'll just use my hands. I haven't had any exercise for some time.

HARRY

Just do it quickly and efficiently. And don't leave any traces.
When you put everything together, the page looks like this.

INT. SCHOOL HALL. DAY
  The platform of a hall in an upper class girl's school. Photos of former governors and head mistresses around the wall. The HEADMISTRESS, aged 52, elegant, slim, addresses the girls at their prize giving. She is flanked by THE PRIME MINISTER, a self-satisfied pompous man of sixty.

HEADMISTRESS

Sir Michael needs little introduction. A man who has excelled in everything he has done . . .
  She looks down at her notes, and is interrupted by scruffy looking nineteen year old DAVE, who burst onto the platform.

DAVE
. . . like murdering us poor sods here and calling it British justice.

Camera directions. Many novice writers fill their scripts with camera directions and advice to the actors. Don't. That's the task of the director. If you want that job, fine, but for the moment you are just the writer.

But where does your job end? You've envisaged the script in a definite way, and though you acknowledge the director's function, you'd really like him or her to see what you had in mind. Well, you can add to the bare bones of the script, but only cautiously, and only as a hint. While you avoid full camera directions, it's fairly well accepted that the writer may use the following suggestions.

ANGLE ON. This means you want to favor a particular character. Joan is speaking but you indicate that attention should be paid to Dave,

POINT OF VIEW, or P.O.V. Here, the image on the screen is seen from the point of view of one of the characters. John is having an eye operation. We show John on the table for shot 17, and make shot 18 P.O.V. John. This means we want to see the room through John's eyes, blurred, with the doctors gazing down at him.

CLOSE UP, or C.U. This is pretty obvious. It's very important you see Helen's face as she hears about the legacy, or the surgeon's hands as he does the operation, so you write in C.U. Helen, or C.U. hands.

Other script directions. Besides everything we've mentioned above, there are two other abbreviations you'll be using quite frequently: O.S. and V.O.

O.S. or O.C. stands for OFF SCREEN or OFF CAMERA. We use these abbreviations when we hear a character but don't actually see him on the screen.

V.O. is simply VOICE-OVER. Here we are watching some action, usually no one is talking, and we hear a voice without seeing its origin. For example, we are looking at fighting and we hear, V.O., "Those were hard years. Dad was always away. We had little money . . . but we had spirit."

The final directions that you are likely to use are FLASHBACK, MONTAGE, and DREAM SEQUENCE. All these devices are to be used with caution.

Take the "falling in love" montage. We've all seen it in countless forms. They've spent their first night together, now they . . . ride the motorbike in the surf as the sun goes down, try all the rides at the amusement park, take the dawn ferry to Staten Island, and so on. Twenty years ago, that montage worked. Today, it has become a cliché.

A last hint. Once, setting the page according to all the screenwriting conventions was difficult and tiresome. Recently, a number of screenwriting software packages have come on the market that will take care of most of your formatting problems. Two of the best are Final Draft and Movie Magic, but you have many other options. Some of the packages can also be downloaded for free.

COMMENCING THE SCRIPT

Breaking the Ice

You've got your story, and you've done your research. You've also thought about plot, structure, and conflict. You know all about formats, and you may even have written a treatment. Don't be surprised, however, if there is a certain reluctance to start putting words on paper. In spite of all your preparations, there can be a psychological barrier about this final test. Don't worry. Everyone faces it and overcomes it.

This is the point where it's worthwhile relaxing for a bit. You know, if you can get the first few lines down, all will be fine. Well, let's think. You know roughly what your first scene is, because you've already set it down in your outline. What was it about? Oh, yes, Cambridge University, in the middle of the nineteenth century. Next, ask yourself a few questions. What do you want to establish? A mood of indolence, idleness, luxury, and money. That should be easy. And what else? That linguist Edward Palmer is going to unknown Sinai.

None of this is difficult. What you have to do is visualize the scene before you write it. If you've done some location research, that shouldn't be difficult. Cambridge . . . what does it conjure up? River. Girls. Men in formal teaching gowns. Green lawns. College spires. Picnics. So you give your brain a push and jump in, and it doesn't matter if this first attempt isn't very good, because you're going to go back and revise it later. But you must get started somewhere, so let's dive in.

1: EXT. CAMBRIDGE UNIVERSITY 1865. DAY
 A large bright spring day at Cambridge. The river Cam runs in front of us, and a couple laze in a boat. Behind them couples walk arm in arm in the college gardens, while an old-fashioned cricket match proceeds in the background. As we hear shouts of "jolly good" and "well played, sir" the camera moves into the glass windows of a magnificent college. This is KING's college. Now we hear another voice emerge over the sounds of the cricket.

JAMISON (V.O.)
But tell me, sir. This crackpot scheme. What will you get out of it?

2: INT. KING'S COLLEGE. DAY

JAMISON (CONT'D.)
You'll be away a year. Your students will forget you. The academy will forget you. Even your patrons at the Bible Society will forget you. For what? . . . a few bits of pottery and a heathen's ring.
 PALMER smiles through all this. He is a handsome man, well over six feet, with an air of cheerful authority.

> PALMER
>
> Ah, Professor, where is your spirit of adventure? Can't you feel the Sinai beckoning? Think of yourself. Six in the morning, gazing down on the sands of time . . . before you the black tents of the nomads, behind you maybe the very rock that Moses struck. And you are standing where no Englishman has been. Isn't that better than teaching Chaucer to nice Christian gentlemen?

3: EXT. BEDOUIN CAMP. DAY

Three BRITISH OFFICERS are sitting on rocks in the middle of an oasis. Sweat is pouring off them, and they continually drink from mess canteens. A fourth officer, BERKELEY rides up on a camel, dismounts and walks slowly towards the group.

> CAPTAIN
>
> Any traces . . . ? Anything?

> BERKELY
>
> Nothing, sir. They tracked him as far as Wadi Arrah, and then lost him.

> CAPTAIN
>
> Wadi Arrah? Damn the bloody fool of a man. What does he think he's on, a picnic in Hyde Park?

And so you go on, scene by scene, till the end of the script. Continually, you'll be asking yourself, does this scene strike the right note? Has it got the element of tension I want? Does it advance the action or just provide atmosphere? Does it set up the action to come? You won't know all the answers, but it is the questioning that counts.

OUTLINES VERSUS SCRIPTS

Your outline is a plan for something that has yet to be born or created. It's a sketch. A guide that shows you the possibilities and the problems, but it is not the work itself. Your script will have an independent life that your treatment can only hint at, and that independence has to be respected.

As you write, your characters come alive on the page, and they and their dialogue and actions will assume a reality you couldn't even dream about. What you have to do is go with the new reality and be ready to diverge from the treatment. If later the script doesn't work, then use the treatment to check some of the technical points like structure and action points. Unless you put the treatment slightly aside, you will never learn to respect your new-born creation.

APPROACH

Scriptwriting is a little like long-distance running. The first time out, all you want to do is get to the end. Then, gradually, you start improving your time and having fun. So don't worry about your first or second script. Just do them. Jump in and write. Take some chances. Have a ball. Then read the scripts and try acting as your own critic. And ask yourself Is this the best, or could I have done better? Is this fine, or could it be improved?

There will be endless revisions, some of your own accord, some arising from script conferences. You will be asked to rewrite, and then rewrite on top of that. It will happen both before and during production. It will seem as if the process never ends, but then the day comes when the film is finished and you see your name up there on the screen. And that moment is worth everything.

PART FOUR
SPECIAL CONSIDERATIONS

10. ADAPTATIONS

Writing adaptations is tricky, problematic, challenging, and fun. And they are very much in demand. *Malcolm X, Citizen Cohn, The Gathering Storm*, and *In the Name of the Father* were all adapted from biographies or autobiographies. *And the Band Played On* and *Barbarians at the Gates* started their lives as best sellers. *My Week with Marilyn* was based on Colin Clarke's diaries entitled *The Prince, The Showgirl and Me*, while the agonizing drama of Aron Ralston's entrapment on a rock face, *127 Hours*, was taken from Ralston's own book *Between a Rock and a Hard Place*. In 2011, an Academy Award nominee, *The Social Network*, was adapted from Ben Mezrich's book *The Accidental Billionaires*.

While books provide the most common source for adaptations, there are numerous other films taken from plays and newspaper articles. So you must learn how to handle this writing technique.

One sees the attraction for the producer. The story has already sold and is highly popular, and the advertising has already been done. When *Diana: Her True Story*, by Andrew Morton, was first published in England, it was sold out in hours, and it repeated that performance in the U.S. Eventually, the screen rights were taken up by Martin Poll Films, and the TV version went on to become one of the highest-rated shows ever, worldwide.

RIGHTS

Before you start work on an adaptation, you must obtain permission to go ahead from the owner of the copyright. There are two ways of doing this:

By making a full purchase of the rights
By taking out an option on the screen rights

An option usually means you have exclusive permission to purchase the rights within a certain amount of time. You normally purchase the full rights only when and if you are absolutely sure the film can and will be made, or if you are scared someone will get in before you. Otherwise you take an option.

You do this because an option costs much less than the full acquisition of the rights. In effect, you are saying, "Give me time to think about the whole project and see if I really want to go ahead with it, or if I can interest someone in it. Then, if everything works out, I will come back and purchase the full rights for an agreed fixed sum at a later date."

In some cases, you may not have to pay for the rights. This is when the work is in the public domain, or the copyright has expired. As the odds are that most of the books and articles you want to adapt will be fairly recent, this proviso about public domain probably won't affect you very much.

The whole question of rights is fairly complex, and I've dealt with it at length in chapter 13. I merely raise the problem here as a warning: don't start adapting anything until you are sure you have rights clearance.

THE TASK OF ADAPTATION

Adapting something means changing it, altering it, modifying it. In screenplay writing, it also means cutting and simplifying. But film achieves its goal in a totally different way from print. You are trying to create a script from which a film will be made that works through visuals, editing, dialogue, music, and effects. In short, you will be creating a totally new form: an *original* screenplay.

There are two approaches to your task. First, you can slavishly follow the original. You say to yourself, "What's in the book, dialogue, incident, and so on that is hallowed, and must be in the film." I think this is a recipe for disaster.

Or you can say, "I'm creating something totally new. The original work is my jumping-off point. I'll be faithful to its spirit and feeling. But I'm working in a different medium that requires different solutions and techniques to bring the work to life for a different audience."

MINDSET

Before you start work on an adaptation, you have to get in the right frame of mind. You've probably read the book a few times, and your head is full of details, incidents, and so on. Now, the time has come to let go. You have to cut the umbilical cord to the original work.

Your first task is put a distance between yourself and the details. Ask yourself broad questions. What moved you in the book? What feelings were you left with? What was the essence of the book? You ask these questions because you want to evoke the same feelings and reactions in your film.

You know from the start you are going to have to lose masses of the book. Whole chapters, incidents, and characters will disappear. Other sections will be reordered. Characters will be combined and dialogue invented. Then you have to remind yourself that the three-and-a-half-hour play, or the thousand-page book, has to be fitted into a two-hour screenplay. So your scissors will be busy.

MEDIA DIFFERENCES

Books and Biographies

Books work through words and accumulation of detail. Often there is little action. Pages are often spent setting out background, atmosphere, character, memories. Books examine psychology and motivation. They wander into the philosophical. They ask questions. They digress, and frequently the manner of the narration is more important than the story.

You can easily see the problems. So you can see why your work goes beyond modification, and will involve you in creating something new.

Plays

Though not as ample a source as books, the theater has also provided rich material for docudrama. Here, the best-known recent example is *Frost/Nixon*. Adapted by Peter Morgan from his 2006 play chronicling the President Nixon and David Frost interviews of 1977, the film received five Academy Award nominations. Not bad by any score.

Your key problem regarding plays is you are adapting a work into a new form. You are going from a medium dominated by words into one dominated by images. This has two implications. First, what works in one form doesn't necessarily work in the other. Second, different forms use different techniques for the same idea. Plays depend on dialogue, and a certain magical relationship between the players and the audience. They can examine the particular, such as a triangle situation in a Noel Coward play, or the human condition, as in the Greek plays.

Generally, theater works best examining character relationships and the small, intimate, personal problems of people. The immediate story may reflect a much larger problem, but it never loses its own particularity. So while Mamet's *Oleanna* provoked a wide debate on the nature of feminism, it always remained grounded in the story of the university professor and his student.

Plays are generally limited in action and setting. A murder can take place but not the invasion of Iraq. Place can change, but only to a limited extent.

Films work in a totally different way. They take advantage of space, and the capacity for broad action. They tend to make their points visually, as much as through dialogue. And they have the resources of special effects, editing, and shot selection to hand.

One of the greatest changes involved in translating plays into films is *opening up*. In the Shakespeare's play *Much Ado about Nothing*, a messenger says of Don Pedro, "He is near. He was not three leagues off when I left him." A page later, he says, "Don Pedro is approached," and the Don enters.

How is this simple dialogue translated into action in Kenneth Branagh's film? We see galloping horses, close-ups of hooves, women racing through bedrooms, showers taken in haste, finery buttoned in passion, until two perspiring, wide-eyed, eager groups of men and women confront each other. The sequence creates a wonderful breathless start to the film, and is all suggested by the words "He is near . . . not three leagues off."

Articles

The general problem with newspaper and magazines articles is that we usually have masses of information, but no clear story. Often there's a complex situation, an abundance of characters, intricate details, but no sense of a clear line that will guide us dramatically through an entertaining story.

While I was researching this book, I collected a number of articles on two public scandals. One involved a bank, and the second the sale of weapons parts to Iran. Both ideas looked very promising; then I found both subjects were too complex. There were no heroes, no clear beginnings, no clear endings. From a journalism point of view, each new revelation made fascinating reading, but it was all too dense for a film.

In contrast, I looked at a *Sunday Times* article about Mordecai Vanunu, the Israeli atom spy. Here, the story was clear and defined. A man had pinched atomic secrets and was pursued by the Israeli secret service. There were only two or three major characters. There was a love story, suspense, and a clear beginning and end. So making a film from the article would have been the easiest thing possible, and of course, someone did.

METHOD

An adaptation is an original screenplay. The source material is merely your jumping-off point. But where do you begin?

Well, first I begin to think seriously about budget. I have to do this because usually the budget will be higher for a feature film than for a TV movie. So I have to be aware of those parameters.

I then reread the text with various colored pencils in hand, a great method suggested by William Goldman. Good dialogue I might mark with red in the margin. A good sequence I mark with blue. Interesting details I might mark with green, and so on. All the time I'm trying find the spine of the film. When you've finished, you should know roughly where you begin and end, and what you've left out.

Then, of course, comes another process. What should you put in to flesh out the film?

What scenes or dialogue can you add that weren't in the book but that would be necessary to make a good film? I then take a yellow legal pad and transfer the notes in an orderly fashion to the paper, adding my own reactions and additional thoughts to the material.

Once I've made the breakdown, I begin to consider four problematic areas in more detail: story, structure, characters, and cutting, and creating.

Story

Often your original material presents you with too many goodies. You have stories galore, and you don't know which one to choose. This was the main problem for the filmmakers tackling *A Bridge Too Far*. The film is about the disastrous battle fought by the British paratroopers for possession of the Arnhem bridges in Holland in 1944 and was scripted by William Goldman. This is how Goldman writes about it in his autobiography.

> Our problem was trying to find a story line. The Cornelius Ryan book is well over 650 pages of print. It's filled with fabulous material . . . but which story to tell. There were so damn many. . . . There were too many incidents that cried out for inclusion—*five* Victoria crosses were awarded for heroism. Surely I needed those five. . . .
> None of the main characters died . . . so I began to fiddle with trying to make some small, instantly sympathetic roles—so that I could have someone to kill in the story. Goddam, though, which story.

Goldman says that his problem was solved when he lucked into structure. Suddenly he realized that for all its complexity, *Bridge* was a cavalry-to-the-rescue story in which the cavalry fails to arrive.

> That was my spine, and anything that wouldn't cling to it I couldn't use. All five Victoria crosses fell out of the picture. Super material went by the boards. But it had to.

There it is. You have to make choices. Something has to go. Find your key story, and junk what distracts you. Sometimes, you may have time for a minor story or a subplot, but view it very carefully. Is your main story in place, and will it stay in place even if you weave things around it? It will? OK, then you can go ahead.

Furthermore, your story may be clear, but you still may not be sure *how* to tell it. Through whose eyes should we view the proceedings? This is a problem we discussed at length in regard to *Exxon Valdez*, where the story was carried by Dan Lawn and Frank Iarossi.

If your protagonist is not clear from the original story, then you may have to hunt a bit to find the right leading character. The problem usually arises when the original work tells the stories of dozens of people, but no one seems to have any centrality.

However, at that juncture you've already done some cutting and simplifying. Out of five possible stories and threads, you've decided what your main story is. You then hunt for one or two characters who can carry it in the best way. Or you combine one or two characters, creating a composite who can carry the story line.

Another decision you occasionally have to make is whether or not to keep the voice and viewpoint of the original, or change it. Again, your actions will be determined solely by what makes for a better film. Kazuo Ishiguro's fine novel *The Remains of the Day* is related by its hero, a butler, Mr. Stevens, who is very prone to reflection and self-questioning. In the film, this first-person voice is rightly abandoned. Instead, we view the man from the outside. We don't need the inner voice, because his filmic deeds and interaction with people now reveal the man so clearly.

Structure

Good films need a good structure. To achieve this you may have to throw overboard a great deal of your original material. On this score, William Goldman cites several problems he had in adapting and scripting *All the President's Men*. As he puts it, "The book had no structure that jumped out at me. And very little dialogue. I also couldn't take great liberties with the material [because everyone was familiar with the story.]"

Goldman's crucial decision was to throw away the last half of the book. In his opinion, the main filmic interest in the story ended after a mistake of Woodward and Bernstein regarding the handling of Haldeman. He then asked Woodward to list for him the most important events in the story, in the order in which they happened. All were contained in the first half of the book, so the junking process was justified.

Goldman's script also illustrates one other thing: the difference in the way you start a book and the way you start a film. The book opens with a sketch of life in Nixon's Washington. And the film? Right! It starts off with the break-in at the Watergate complex. You don't waste time. You just get straight in there.

Where beginnings can be hard is when you're adapting intricate biographies, and complex medical, industrial, and disaster stories. This is because the book writer has had time to play around with background, atmosphere, and history before he or she gets into the main story. But you can't do that. In film, you have to move in fast and grab the audience.

This means that in a film about Churchill, you ignore what the book said about his grandfather building an estate and plunge straight into the hero's career in the army. Similarly, in a film about bin Laden, you might start off with a terrorist attack rather than dwell on his early schooling.

When you adapt a book, beware of your change of audience. The book was possibly a minority taste, bought by only a few people with a prior interest in the subject. Your film, however, aims at a mass audience, and you have to draw them into your subject from the start. That means if they know nothing about the subject, you have to provide context and background immediately, as in the case of *Citizen Cohn*.

HBO's film *Citizen Cohn* is based on the biography of Roy Cohn by Nicholas von Hoffman. Cohn was a lawyer in the 1950s and is today probably unknown to many people under the age of sixty. This problem of identification, recognition, and interest was solved by creating two introductory sequences.

The first shows a montage of U.S. news footage from the 1950s. The emphasis is on the Cold War, the fight against communism, the fear of atomic warfare, the rise of McCarthyism, and the pursuit of Reds. So very briefly, we are given the spirit of the times.

The next sequence takes place in a hospital. It's 1986, and a man is dying. A nurse and doctor hover round the bed.

> NURSE
>
> Who is this guy?

> YOUNG DOCTOR
>
> The White House rang. The President wanted to know what he could do for him.

> SENIOR DOCTOR
>
> Probably wanted to make sure he was dead.

> DOCTOR
>
> Did you know this guy?

> SENIOR DOCTOR
>
> We knew him all right. Joe McCarthy's right-hand man.

> DOCTOR
>
> My father said he was a great patriot . . .

> SENIOR DOCTOR
>
> Great patriot . . . ?

> DOCTOR
>
> The spies. The Rosenbergs. He got them executed.

> SENIOR DOCTOR
>
> Well twenty dollars says the great patriot doesn't make it till dawn.

> COHN
>
> (rising up from bed) Fuck you!

We are now really hooked by the sequence. Who is this man that the president feared, who was the right-hand man of the hated Joe McCarthy, and who got men executed? We want to know more, and suddenly we are into the body of the picture.

Cutting and Creating

The art of adaptation is dominated by two things: the need to cut and the need to invent.

Cutting is easiest. You cut out irrelevant scenes, chapters, characters, incidents, until you have a malleable story with a clear focus. Creating is the other side of the coin. Here, you may need to write in incidents and scenes that were only hinted at in the book. You may also have to amalgamate characters, or create new ones. And you most definitely will have to create dialogue.

If you're lucky, much of the dialogue will appear in your source material, or be available from diaries, witnesses, and reports. It will often be stilted, and your task then is to take the essence of the dialogue and turn it in to simple conversational English. As we mentioned in earlier discussions of dialogue, it must be appropriate to the person's attitude, style, and opinions.

You will also frequently amalgamate characters, and that has to be done with great care. If a number of doctors are equally involved in inventing a new drug and none are in the public eye or well known, you would have a case for fictionalizing them, or amalgamating them into one. If a particular doctor was more prominent, or claimed to have discovered the drug by himself, then you would probably leave him as he was.

These decisions aren't easy. There are few rules, and every case has to be judged on its own merits.

Since the problem of fictionalization is so tricky, and can create immense legal difficulties, most networks issue guidelines on the subject. For example, they will require information about composite or fictional characters in your script to make sure there is no claim for accidental identification. The guidelines are worth looking at, and I've reprinted a copy of the NBC rules in appendix A.

THE PROCESS IN PRACTICE

In order to show you how the art of adaptation works in practice, I've chosen three books and their film scripts as examples for further analysis. I've also taken a quick look at the film *The Social Network*, based on *The Accidental Billionaires*, by Ben Mezrich.

Diana: Her True Story and *Barbarians at the Gates* were nonfiction best sellers that gave birth to two very successful television productions. *Public Enemies*, for its part, provided the basis for an excellent gangster film. All three books and their screenplays are very different and, examined together, illustrate many of the problems and possibilities of adaptation.

Diana: Her True Story

When Andrew Morton's book *Diana: Her True Story* came out, Diana was still alive, public interest in her at its height, and the book became an instant best seller. Later, it was made into a TV miniseries by Martin Poll films, with a script by Stephen Zito.

On the whole, the book follows the film very faithfully, but there is one alteration of emphasis that is very important. In the book, Camilla Parker-Bowles (now Prince Charles's wife) is merely one element of anxiety for Diana among many. In the film, however, she comes very much to the fore as one of the principal causes for Diana's jealousy and insecurity.

Below, I've extracted sections from the book, together with various script sequences, so that you can see in detail the relationship of one to the other. I've also tried to point out the rationale for some of the changes and have underlined dialogue passages from the script that are taken straight from the book.

Beginning. Both book and film start from the same point.

It was a memory engraved upon her soul. . . . She could hear her father loading suitcases into the boot of a car, then Frances, her mother, crunching across the gravel forecourt, the clunk of a car door being shut, and the sound of a car engine revving and fading as her mother drove through the gates of Park House and out of her life. Diana was six years old.

In the film we get the same scene, almost detail for detail. A six-year-old Diana sits at the bottom of the staircase. She hears a car drive away, and her father enters.

> EARL SPENCER
> Don't worry, darling. Everything will be all right.

> DIANA
> When will Mummy be coming back?

> EARL SPENCER
> She doesn't want to live with us, Diana. Not any longer.

> DIANA
> (in tears) She didn't even kiss me goodbye.

The book then devotes a chapter to Diana's early years. This is all cut out of the film except for a few nursery and holiday sequences. The atmosphere is taken from the book, but one obviously invented element is added, a small but pertinent question of her grandmother's as they watch the royal family on TV.

> LADY FERMOY
> Tell me, Diana. What would you like to be when you grow up?

> DIANA
> A ballet dancer or a princess.

> SARAH SPENCER
> Diana, you're such a ninny.

> LADY FERMOY
> Sarah! The first Lady Diana Spencer almost married the Prince of Wales two and a half centuries ago.

> DIANA
> Didn't he love her, Grandma . . . ?
> Diana looks at Charles on the TV.

> DIANA
> He has such funny ears.

The scene also introduces us to Lady Fermoy. In the book, she is a very incidental character, but in the film, her part is enlarged. She becomes Diana's confidante but is also shown as being very close to the queen, so that we can get the royal view of the relationship.

Scene Expansion. In the second chapter, we are told a little bit more about Diana and are given some information about a number of Charles's girlfriends, one of whom was Diana's elder sister. The book then goes on: While their romance cooled off, Charles still asked Sarah [Diana's sister] to attend his 30th birthday party at Buckingham Palace in November 1978. Much to Sarah's surprise Diana was also invited. Cinderella was going to the ball.

The book then says that Diana enjoyed herself immensely and moves on to another topic. However, the setting of the party is too good for the scriptwriter to miss, and the *expansion* takes up five pages of the script. Diana sees the party as something out of a fairytale. Her sister tells us Charles is a romantic but never stays in love very long. Lord Mountbatten, Charles's uncle, talks to him about love, and the queen mother talks to Diana. It's the first "big scene" in the film and presents a chance to meet the principal characters.

It also inserts a dramatic point, but one that is absent from the book. According to author Andrew Morton, Charles's escort for the evening was actress Susan George. In the film, there is no mention of the actress; instead, Charles dances with Camilla, who will be Diana's rival for years.

CAMERA ON CHARLES DANCING WITH CAMILLA

CAMILLA
Well, Fred. See anything here that catches your eye?

CHARLES
Yes, I'm holding her in my arms.

Dialogue Roots. As is clear, most of the dialogue is made up. Even with friends present, it is highly unlikely we would know what Charles whispered to Camilla.

Morton's book contains very little dialogue, and where it does, it usually mentions the source. Where possible, Zito, the scriptwriter, incorporate known conversations into the script. *Hints* at conversations also get expanded in the script, though sometimes put into the mouths of different people. So, on page 48 of the book, we find the following passage:

Unfortunately for Charles his title brought obligations as well as privileges. His duty was to marry and produce an heir to the throne. It was a subject Earl Mountbatten discussed endlessly with the Queen during afternoon tea at Buckingham Palace, while Prince Phillip let it be known that he was growing impatient with his son's irresponsible approach to marriage.

A lot of this passage is transferred to the film, but put directly into the mouth of Lord Mountbatten, Charles's uncle.

CHARLES
The problem is, Uncle Dicky, that most girls don't see me for what I am. I tend to scare the really nice ones away.

LORD MOUNTBATTEN

Quite right. But don't imagine that because you've become a sort of Royal pop idol that the British people will always support you. They'll back you only so long as you serve the country. *And part of your duty to the nation is to marry and produce an heir.* The people need to be assured the monarchy will continue.

We also find this in the book:

> The Prince, then nearly 33 . . . had publicly acknowledged the problems of finding a suitable bride. "Marriage is a much more important business than falling in love. . . . Essentially you must be good friends, and love, I'm sure, will grow out of that friendship. I have a particular responsibility to ensure that I make the right decision. The last thing I could possibly entertain is getting divorced."
>
> On another occasion he declared that marriage was a partnership where his wife was not simply marrying a man but a way of life. . . . Marriage in his eyes was primarily the discharge of an obligation to his family and the nation, a task made all the more difficult by the immutable nature of the contract.

These lines of Charles's and the comments of Morton finally find their way into the film script in a courting scene between Charles and Diana in the gardens of Bolehyde Manor.

CHARLES

When a man in my position marries, the choice must be made very carefully. It has to be someone special . . . someone who can fulfill the role. I think you are lucky if you find the person attractive in the physical sense as well as the mental, but marriage is basically a very strong partnership, Diana, a partnership.

DIANA

You've certainly given this matter considerable thought.

CHARLES

A woman not only marries a man: she marries into a way of life—a job. She's got to have some knowledge of it.

Suggested Scenes. Shortly after the book's discussion of Charles's marital needs, there is a short description of a house party in the country. This is the setting for a meeting between Charles and Diana that deepens their intimacy and propels them toward marriage. Lord Mountbatten's murder at the hands of the IRA is merely mentioned in passing in the book, as can be seen from this passage.

> Diana was seated next to Charles on a bale of hay and, after the usual pleasantries, the conversation moved on to Earl Mountbatten's death, and his funeral in Westminster Abbey. In a conversation, which

she later recalled to friends, Diana told him: "You looked so sad when you walked up the aisle at the funeral. My heart bled for you when I watched. I thought, it's wrong. You are lonely. You should be with somebody to look after you."

This casual mention of Mountbatten's death, however, provides the opportunity for Zito to develop three important sequences.

35A. EXT. BALMORAL. DAY

Charles is out shooting. He fires both barrels at a bird on the wing. He hits nothing and stops in his tracks. He shivers with more than the cold.

As a premonition hits him, he looks up to see his father coming towards him. One look at Phillip's face and Charles knows something is wrong.

PRINCE PHILIP

(Gravely) We've come from Ireland.

CHARLES

Uncle Dicky?

PRINCE PHILIP

Yes. The IRA.

CHARLES

Those bastards!

From there we move to Westminster Abbey to see the funeral itself.

42: INT. WESTMINSTER ABBEY. DAY

Charles movingly delivers a eulogy for his beloved uncle.

CHARLES

The quality of real moral courage, of being able to face unpleasant tasks that need to be done—and yet to be fair and consistent—is a rare quality indeed.

CLOSE ON Diana who, with Sarah and Jane, is among the mourners. She can't take her eyes off Charles. His grief and dignity move her deeply.

CHARLES

But he had it in abundance. That's why people would have followed him into hell. It is also one of the reasons I adored him and why so many of us miss him dreadfully now.

This scene, which is not in the book, makes two very important contributions to the drama. First, it shows us Diana's growing feeling for Charles. Clearly, she imagines Charles as having many of the same qualities as Mountbatten and can also see people following him to hell. Equally important, it shows us a human, vulnerable side of Charles that is missing for most of the film.

In a quoted book passage, Morton also mentions discussion of "the usual pleasantries" and gives a brief quote of Diana's recollection of the funeral. In the film, the few lines are transformed by Zito into a major courting scene, the end of which is set out below.

Charles takes a long look at Diana. She's become an attractive young woman. Sweet and full of life. He's pleased at her good manners and breeding.

> CHARLES
> One feels secure around you, Diana. I think my uncle might have approved of you.

> DIANA
> Lord Mountbatten must have been a terrible loss for you.

> CHARLES
> (touched by her sympathy) I adored him and miss him so dreadfully now. (growing quiet) he was more like a father . . . he always had time for me.

> DIANA
> I know exactly what you mean. My grandmother's the one I depend on to set me on the right path. (full of sympathy) *You looked so sad at the funeral. I thought "It's wrong. You are lonely. You should be with someone to look after you."*
> Her words have touched a deep chord. Charles sees her with new eyes.

> CHARLES
> (flirting) well, somebody had better had.
> He gives her a smile that says, "Are you interested in applying for the job?"

Selection and Ordering. At the beginning of chapter 5 of his book, Morton details Diana's increasing depression after marriage, and the failure of Charles to understand or help.

> On that January day in 1982, her first New Year within the royal family, she now threatened to take her own life. Charles accused her of crying wolf, and prepared to go riding. She was as good as her word. Standing on top of the wooden staircase she hurled herself to the ground, landing in a heap at the bottom . . .
> The incident was one of many domestic crises which crowded in upon the royal couple in those tumultuous early days. . . . On one occasion she threw herself against a glass display cabinet at Kensington Palace, while on another she slashed her wrists with a razor blade. During a heated argument with Charles she picked up a penknife lying on his dressing table and cut her chest and thighs. Although she was bleeding her husband studiously scorned her.

The note about throwing herself down the stairs, and other actions of Diana obviously offered Stephen Zito terrific dramatic possibilities, which he translates into film as follows:

212. INT. WINDSOR CASTLE. STAIRWAY. DAY
    Charles is dressed for hunting. Diana rushes after him.

> DIANA
>
> I can't take any more of this, Charles. I swear I'm going to do something drastic.

> CHARLES
>
> Why don't you just come along?

> DIANA
>
> Because standing in the mud watching you kill innocent animals for sport isn't my idea of spending time together.
>> Charles, at a loss, starts to go.

> DIANA
>
> What about me?

> CHARLES
>
> What about you? (exploding) All I had to do was marry and produce an heir. And wait for my turn to be King.

> DIANA
>
> You have a wife.

> CHARLES
>
> Yes. So I am reminded.
>> He turns his back on her. We move with him.

> DIANA (V.O.)
>
> Charles.
>> He whirls around to see Diana tumbling down the stairs, crashing hard into the railing. She lies as still as death.

FADE TO BLACK

The scene is beautifully written in terms of providing a dramatic build up to Diana's suicide attempt and also acts as a climax to the first part of the film. However, as I've indicated, the book immediately goes on to list other cries for help.

The problem this presents to a writer is whether to use any more incidents, and if so, *which one* and *when*. The book lumps everything together, but to do so and crowd everything together in a film would be to lose dramatic impact. Wisely, Zito holds of the second incident and crisis until a *good deal later* in the script. Here the scene is placed in Diana and Charles's breakfast room at Highgrove. Charles has just told Diana he is not going to give up Camilla Parker-Bowles.

> CHARLES
>
> I don't intend to give her up altogether. So you'd better get used to it.
>> Charles starts out of the room.

> DIANA
>
> I'm *not* going to get used to it, Charles.

Diana, in helpless frustration, smashes her arm against a china cabinet. The glass shatters. A shard cuts Diana. Charles rushes to her and looks down at her bloody arm.

CHARLES

Damn you, Diana.
The servants have rushed in and look horrified.

CHARLES

The Princess has had another accident.

The delay in showing the second incident helps the pacing of the story line. When the accident does happen, it provides one more link in the deteriorating domestic situation. Had it been placed closer to the stairs fiasco (as in the book), it would have lost most of its effect.

Another point to note is that Zito adds *motivation* for Diana's actions by bringing in Camilla. In the book, all we know is that Charles and Diana are having a hard time.

Finally, it's worth noting a line from the book that Morton quotes from one of Diana's friends. "His indifference pushed her to the edge, whereas he could have romanced her to the edge of the world." It's only one sentence, but it governs the whole mood of the scene and gets its filmic expression in "Damn you, Diana."

Barbarians at the Gate

Barbarians at the Gate: The Fall of RJR Nabisco was written by Bryan Burrough and John Helyar. The book describes the fight for control of the gigantic food and tobacco company in 1988. It was a best seller and, along with *Liar's Poker*, paints a damning portrait of greed and lust on Wall Street.

In spite of its fame, the book doesn't immediately strike you as material for a film. Its subject is the competition to take over a major American company, using a leveraged buyout, or LBO. The main action of the book takes place in boardrooms and banks. We are introduced to an esoteric financial world, and given immense detail about the way it works. Soon the mind reels as you grapple with the intricacies of junk bonds, asset stripping, stock resets, and tax loopholes. Not too promising for a film.

However, *Barbarians* also reveals human lust, desire, and avarice at their worst. It talks of a world where forty million dollars can be made in an hour, for just waiting around. It appalls us, and it fascinates us, and, as more than one producer knew, it might just be a great basis for a movie, if the right scriptwriter could be found.

The eventual choice was Larry Gelbart, who among other things had done the final script for *Tootsie*. The film itself was made by HBO and received a very high rating. Though production and direction were fine, to my mind most of the film's success was due to Gelbart's brilliant adaptation. Below I've set out some of his strategies in bringing such a complex book to the screen.

Aim and Direction. The original book is a serious intricate study of the *company takeover* process. To a large extent, though obviously not completely, the film ignores the details of the *process* and concentrates on the *players.* This is a film about people, greed, and rivalry; and discussions about bonds and percentages stay where they belong, on the financial pages.

The other radical change is that the film is set up as a *comedy,* which occasionally borders on farce. The book hints at this possibility but stays on the right side of seriousness. What Gelbart does is pick up the suggestions and then vault over the barrier into the laughter section, adjacent to situation comedy.

The Conflict. In both book and film, the structure of the dramatic conflict evolves very easily. Essentially, there are two sides in the takeover battle: the management team, led by Ross Johnson; and their opponents, Kravis, Kohlberg, and Roberts, led by Henry Kravis. The prize is ownership of RJR Nabisco, and whoever wins is likely to make hundreds of millions of dollars in profit.

In the book, there are dozens of contestants and multiple shenanigans to take over the companies. What the film script does is simplify the struggle, without losing the spirit of the book. Purists may regret this, but I think Gelbart was absolutely right in his choice. With four or five contestants, the race becomes blurred. With only two giants struggling against each other, the issues are clear and emotionally much more compelling.

Gelbart's structural model could have been the baseball film centered around the World Series. There is a prize, and two sides battle it out. The point here is that the audience has clear genre expectations. It goes to see romantic comedies, sci-fi, action films, and buddy movies knowing more or less how things will evolve, and it derives satisfaction from variations on old themes. Making your adaptation fit into a genre type often helps in regard to audience acceptance. Here it helps enormously to see a possibly off-putting financial struggle framed in terms that everyone can understand.

The Hero. The book offers us a number of central characters, but no central "hero." Realizing he needs one, Gelbart chooses Ross Johnson, the CEO of Nabisco and leader of the management buyout group, and puts him center stage.

Johnson is a breezy, outgoing character with a beautiful young wife, Laurie, and a penchant for telling dirty jokes. This we know from the book, which tells us as well about his love for corporate luxuries, such as his jet fleet. We also know he is money hungry and has arranged for himself and his close friends to make over fifty million dollars if they win.

Gelbart knows, however, that some of these characteristics can be off-putting to an audience. He compensates for this by giving Ross some very funny lines, and making him very concerned for the future of his workers. We very warm to Ross, but he's not exactly the man as seen in the book. Gelbart's change is vital in gaining audience sympathy for Ross, and making the adaptation work.

Cast Cutting and Amplifying. There are over sixty major characters in the book. Gelbart wisely reduces this cast to six major characters, and five minor ones, with Ross playing the hero, as mentioned, with banker Henry Kravis being his principal opponent.

Gelbart does more than reduce. He also *amplifies* the roles of people hardly mentioned in the book, such as Ross's wife, Laurie, and Kravis's wife, Carolyne. He does this for three reasons. Enlarging the role of the wives allows him to write a number of domestic scenes, which provide intimacy and contrast to the boardroom scenes. The presence of the wives also allows Gelbart to develop a number of sexy bedroom scenes out of his imagination. Finally, the wives also act as the bounce figures for providing vital information to the audience, such as how Ross and Henry feel, what they think of their rivals, and how they see their future game plans.

Settings. Barbarians is about the world of the super-rich, as portrayed in the Fortune 400. This atmosphere, which the book can only hint at, becomes a major factor in the film.

Seventy percent of the action in the book takes place in boardrooms. In the film, Gelbart transforms these conversations to stretch limousines, luxury jets, opulent ballrooms, and grand mansions. In the book, we get a passing remark that Kravis has a 5.5-million-dollar Park Avenue apartment, laden with Renoirs. Taking this hint, Gelbart provides us with a few scenes in Kravis's house that tell us once and for all this film is about money, greed, and Croesus-style wealth.

Humor, Invention, and Strategies. The perennial question in doing adaptations is how and where to add to the original book in order to bring the story to life in a different medium. This, of course, is also true, when writing your standard script. Gelbart provides many lessons in this sphere.

First, he creates a number of comic and satirical scenes that were never in the book. The funniest is a fancy-dress ball in the Plaza hotel, where all the principals dress up in the most outlandish costumes from Marie Antoinette to Billy the Kid. Strange encounters on the dance floor are then topped by a madcap scene in the men's toilet, where cowboy figures pop up all over the place, to proposition Ross with buyout offers. This is bedroom farce transferred to a men's urinal.

Another wonderful touch is the creation of Antony, the pizza boy, as a running gag. While delivering a pizza to the boardroom, Antony overhears the conversation. He promptly telephones his broker to sell IBM and buy Nabisco. This is topped at the end of the film when we see Antony, the pizza man, wearing an Armani suit and driving by in a Porsche.

Dialogue. Gelbart never misses an opportunity to expand and change scenes from the book where they give him a chance to create some devastatingly funny and sharp dialogue. Thus, the crushing failure of a new, much-vaunted Premier smokeless cigarette, which is supposed to save the Nabisco company, is exploited to the full for its comic potential.

In the book, the new smokeless cigarette is exhibited as an after-dinner surprise for Ross Johnson's guests at his villa. Someone drops a crack that it smells like burning lettuce. Someone else comments, "Boy, this is hard to draw on."

In the script, the scene is transferred from Ross's home to a testing lab, and goes as follows.

23: INT. RJR REYNOLDS CIGARETTE TESTING LAB. AFTERNOON

Before a huge cross-section mockup of a Premier cigarette, Ross and Horrigan listen to RJR executive TRAVIS GAINES, who is in a white lab coat. Behind him is a pie chart indicating the following figures.

GAINES

Of all the people we interviewed, eighty-six percent approved of the idea of a smokeless cigarette. Forty-one percent said they'd try at least two packs before deciding whether to switch brands. Of those who'd given up cigarettes, seventy-three percent responded favorably to the idea, saying they'd seriously consider smoking again, if they could be positive that the cigarette they were smoking was absolutely smokeless.

Ross loves those numbers.

GAINES

Eight percent of *that* group sampled at least one Premier to give us their opinion of the product.

ROSS (EXPECTANTLY)

Bottom line?

GAINES

Of all the groups we tested, their reaction to Premiers was just about uniform.

Silence.

ROSS

(pleasantly anticipatory) Uh huh . . . ?

Gaines, reluctant to go on, looks at Horrigan.

HORRIGAN

(sheepishly) They all said they tasted like shit.

ROSS

Like shit?

GAINES

Shit was the consensus. Yes, sir.

ROSS

They *all* said that? *Nobody* liked them?

GAINES

Fewer than five percent.

ROSS

(to Horrigan) You said you heard that the results were terrific.

HORRIGAN

Nothing wrong with five percent. I'll take five percent of the smoking market any day of the week.

ROSS

Jesus Christ! How much are we in for up to now?

HORRIGAN

Upwards of seven-fifty.

ROSS

We've spent seven hundred and fifty million dollars and we've come up with a turd with a tip? God Almighty, Ed. We poured enough technology into this project to send a cigarette to the moon, and all we got out of it is one that tastes like it took a dump.

HORRIGAN

(sheepishly again) We haven't even talked about the smell.

ROSS

What'd they say *that* was like? A fart?

HORRIGAN

(unhappily inhales) Yep.

ROSS

You're not serious. That's what they said?

1ST SCIENTIST

We've got an awful lot of fart figures, sir.

ROSS

Tastes like shit, and smells like a fart. We've got ourselves a real winner here. It's one God damn unique advertising slogan. I'll give you that. Seven hundred and fifty million dollars.
[That's not the end of Ross's troubles, as he finds out a few moments later.]

ROSS

(taking a drag) And what the hell's wrong with the draw? You need an extra pair of lungs to take a drag.

1ST SCIENTIST

It's what we call the "hernia effect."

ROSS

Oh, is that what we call it? There's *another* great billboard. What do we do? Give away a truss with every pack? "Warning. This cigarette can tear your balls off."

Public Enemies

Public Enemies was a 2009 film directed by Michael Mann, and written by Mann, Ronan Bennett, and Ann Biderman. Basically, it was adapted from Bryan Burrough's book *Public Enemies,* a very wide-ranging book that covers America's gangster years from 1932 to 1935, and deals with characters as diverse as Bonnie and Clyde, Machine Gun Kelly, Pretty Boy Floyd, Baby Face Nelson, and John Dillinger. It also looks at the rise of the FBI under Herbert Hoover.

Mann's film concentrates on the career of bank robber John Dillinger, and his very choice of making the film surprises us since at least six films have been made on the life of Dillinger. Where Burrough's book differs from other sources on Dillinger's life is the sheer amount of detail that it provides on the gangster's actions and background.

However, it cannot have been an easy book to adapt because Dillinger's biography and other details about him are spread over so many different chapters, some involving Baby Face Nelson, some involving Machine Gun Kelly, others depicting his family, and the depression years.

Also, as you read Burrough's book you sees quickly that Dillinger's life was not very interesting. Basically, it consisted of bank robberies, prison escapes, and fleeing the police. There is no hint of whether and how he enjoyed his money, how he really enjoyed his free time (if any), and no great escapes to Bolivia like Butch Cassidy and the Sundance Kid. Because of this repetition of actions, robbery after robbery, and yet richness of materials, it's interesting to see where the scriptwriters concentrated their efforts.

Storyline. Whereas Burrough's book provides a great deal of information about Dillinger's youth, and his early history, this is entirely left out of the film. So we are not told that he was in the Navy, and deserted, nor that he was briefly married. More important, we are not told about his early robberies, and that he spent over six years incarcerated. Instead, the film elects to concentrate on the last two years of his life, ending with his being shot down by the FBI outside a cinema. A wise decision, which again illustrates the necessity of choosing wisely what to cut out in making an adaptation.

Dramatic Variety. Bang bang. Robbery. Pursuit. Capture. Jailbreak. Robbery. As I've mentioned, the book provides full details of Dillinger's actions, but there's not much variety. To break this banal pattern, the scriptwriters enlarge two elements found here and there in the book, but dispersed over many chapters and pages.

First, Dillinger's affair with Billie Flachette is enlarged to provide a major romantic element of the film. In reality, Billie was a not-too-glamorous hatcheck girl, who became a member of Dillinger's gang. In the film, she becomes an extremely attractive young girl, not too sure of Dillinger's actions, but devotedly in love.

The key change from book to film is that the FBI, and particularly agent Melvin Purvis, now take center stage to provide the necessary opponents for Dillinger. So Purvis's character is filled out in the film, while considerable time is also spent in showing us the expansion of the FBI and Hoover's office in their fight against crime.

Some of this is hinted at in the book but gets full treatment in the film. Of particular interest is J. Edgar Hoover's confrontation with skeptical members of Congress. These scenes are in many ways much more interesting than the standard shoot-out scenes, particularly as they reveal to us how the later fabled Hoover was seen in his early days. So, hidden in the density of the 570-page book, we read the following:

That morning Hoover made his case with an array of statistics, charts and graphs, pointing out that the FBI had all but eliminated kidnappings as a national threat. When he finished, McKellar attacked. . . .

"It seems to me your department is just running wild, Mr. Hoover," McKellar said. "I think, Mr. Hoover, with all the money in your hands you are just extravagant . . ."

They proceeded to quibble over how many cases the FBI had solved. "How many people have been killed by your department since they've been allowed to use guns?" McKellar asked.

"I think there have been eight desperadoes killed by our agents, and we have had four agents in our service killed by them."

"In other words the net effect of turning guns over to your department has been the killing of eight desperadoes and four G-men."

Now clearly seeking to embarrass Hoover McKellar pressed for his qualifications to run the bureau. Hoover pointed out that he had been with the Department of Justice nineteen years.

"Did you ever make an arrest?"

"No, sir; I have investigations."

Hoover mentioned several other cases. "Did you make the arrests?" McKellar asked.

"The arrests were made by . . . officers under my supervision."

In the film, the above passage is enlarged and deepened into the following dialogue:

INT. CONGRESSIONAL HEARING ROOM. J. E. HOOVER. DAY

J. EDGAR HOOVER is a physically short man but has a dynamic presence. He is completely free from self-doubt. He's youthful and 33 years old. MCKELLAR is Chairman of the Senate Appropriations Sub-Committee. He's an avuncular man of 62.

MCKELLAR

So in the middle of a Great Depression you're looking for a budget increase to build up your department. But by my tally your department spends more tax payer's dollars catching crooks than what the crooks you catch stole in the first place . . .

HOOVER

That's ridiculous. The Bureau's apprehended kidnappers, bank robbers, who have stolen up to . . .

MCKELLAR

How many criminals have you apprehended . . . ? I mean you, personally.

HOOVER

I've never arrested anybody. I'm an administrator.

MCKELLAR

With no field experience.

For once Hoover is silent.

MCKELLAR (CONT'D)
In fact you're shockingly unqualified, aren't you sir? You have never personally conducted a criminal investigation in the field in your life.
Others in the room stare at Hoover. McKellar leans back . . .

MCKELLAR (CONT'D)
I think you are a front. I think your prowess as a lawman is a myth created from a hoopla of headlines by your publicist. You are trying to make a federal police force with you set up as its Tsar. . . . Your appropriation request is denied.
[After McKellar's refusal to make an appropriation for Hoover's bureau, Hoover talks to his colleagues as they rush down a corridor. There doesn't seem to be a basis for the remarks in the book, but they seem to be added from what we know of Hoover today.]

HOOVER
(referring to McKellar) Find out. Was he soft on Reds in 1919. Does he use prostitutes? Peppy stuff like that. And feed this to Walter Winchell: "McKellar's a Neanderthal. He's on a personal vendetta to destroy me." Like that . . . We'll fight him on the front page. Not in his damn committee room.

The Social Network

Though it was extremely popular, Ben Mezrich's book *The Accidental Billionaires* doesn't strike you at first as good material for a film. Yes, the subject is fascinating—the shocking expansion of that mass wonder called Facebook—but much of the book takes place in front of computers, while all the talk is of website development and writing the correct codes and algorithms. Yet surprisingly, the film works beautifully.

The reason is that while the film keeps very closely to the dialogue and incidents in the book, it reshapes the order of the sequences, does some judicious cutting, and puts Mark Zuckerberg dead center from the start.

In the book, we spend the first two chapters being introduced to Eduardo Saverin. He has made three hundred thousand dollars on the stock market and will later be Mark's right-hand man. Fine for a book beginning; no good for a film. Instead, the film starts off with Mark having an argument with his girlfriend, who has decided to leave him. Here, we immediately grasp the nature of Mark. Feisty, brusque, abrupt, and not particularly likeable. It's a good scene but comes from the imagination of the scriptwriter, as we learn very early in the book that Mark has no girlfriends.

A large part of the book has to do with the social codes at Harvard, and the importance of getting into the right club or fraternity. The Phoenix is good, but all the masters of the world belong to the Porcellian Club. Most of this is rightly cut, with only a few hints being thrown out here and there about the clubs. This also means that the conditions of Eduardo's acceptance into the Phoenix, such as walking around three days accompanied by a chicken, have to be omitted. In other words, the scriptwriter has decided the film is about the charge forward of Facebook, and all the rest is diversion.

In the book, the Winklevoss twins are introduced very early, rowing on the Charles. In the film, they enter only after twenty minutes, giving us time to get to know Mark and the crazy wild development of his Facemash site.

We talked in an earlier chapter on the need for conflict, and as things progress the quarrel between Mark and the Winklevoss twins (and later Eduardo) provides just such a conflict, after Facebook takes off. And it's here we can see what the craft of good adaptation can do. In the book, events proceed in chronological order. In the film, however, we are suddenly in the midst of a trial hearing between Mark and his opponents. This is already after Facebook has made millions.

While the trial takes place in the present, we get entrancing flashbacks of the events that lead up to the trial. Thus, we have two stories in parallel. It's not a new device, but here works very well.

In one sense, it's hard to understand the success of *The Social Network*, because it conforms to none of the usual norms. It takes place for the most part in dark student rooms, in crowded bars, in the standard university clubs, and around the classrooms and dormitories of Harvard Yard. It has the grace to show the beauty of the Charles River at dawn, and rowing at Henley Royal Regatta. But in the main, it gives us few visual delights.

It also never tries to turn us on sexually. There are a few encounters with girls, but most are very conventional one-night stands. Further, as mentioned above, the dialogue is mostly about computer puzzles, and finance. So why does the film work? Is there a lesson in it about choosing the right materials for an adaptation?

Why did the producers decide to adapt this rather austere book? I think because they realized that while the book had none of the usual ingredients, it was intellectually fascinating, stimulating, and exciting to the imagination. And it had hidden aspects that only gradually revealed themselves. It was a story of rags (almost) to riches.

It was the story of a boy who beat the system, the system being the Harvard administration and the usual social constraints. And dealing as it did with the Internet, and with social connections, it was the perfectly timed story for our day and age, telling us, subconsciously, that if Mark can make it, we might, too.

Adaptations are tricky, but interesting, and for exercise you might want to think about a book you would like to adapt and how you would do it. After rereading it a few times, start considering what sections you'd lose. Are you happy with the story and its shape? Are there sections or incidents you think would work well visually? Are there scenes or hints of scenes you think you could expand? Are you happy with the characters? Which ones do you want to carry the story? Which ones do you have to abandon? What characters might you combine? Does the hero need a confidante or a buddy? And so you go on, even writing a few scenes with dialogue. Is it fascinating? Yes! I think so! And if you try it, I think you'll agree.

11. PRINT THE LEGEND?

When challenged about the veracity of an incident in one of his films, the director John Ford is reputed to have said something like, "When it's fact against legend, print the legend." If questioned about truth and fiction in docudrama today, one suspects he would also have said, "To hell with the truth, go for the drama."

Can drama and reality make a happy marriage? Well, as Hamlet might have said, if he'd been around today, that's the $64,000 question. While docudrama is tremendously popular, it has also drawn in the wrath of a number of critics. Thus Jerry Kuehl, one of the most serious opponents of the form, wrote this for the English magazine *Vision*.

> Most docudramas are produced with little regard for historical truth, or psychological plausibility, but with every regard for pecuniary advantage. To see the names of real people with public reputations attached to characters drawn from the stockpile of drama stereotypes . . . is enough to alert the viewer that he or she is in the presence of a program which intends to exploit but not satisfy an audience's curiosity.

At the end of season 1 of TV's popular series *Mad Men*, the boss of the advertising firm hears a devastating revelation about Don Draper. His reaction is, Who cares? Similarly, we might ask, Should we take Kuehl's remarks seriously? I personally believe it is useful for the writer to listen to the critics, so that he or she knows what troubles serious thinkers about docudrama or its execution.

TRUTH OR FICTION

Writing docudrama, as I've said, is like boxing with one hand tied behind your back, and the rope that binds you is called "truth." To reach the rewards, you have to be prepared to live dangerously, and at every step you have to recall the sign over the entrance to the minefield: "Watch the facts."

The key problem for docudrama lies in its relationship to truth and to audience expectation. Can imaginative drama really exist when its hands are shackled by the bonds of accuracy? Not everyone believes historical veracity and truth are necessarily the most important guidelines to the form. Thus, Nigel Andrews, an English newspaper critic, argues very persuasively for exactly the opposite view.

> If cinema cannot play fast and loose with history should it bother to play with it at all? . . . Look at the strength freedom with truth gave to some truth based films: *Bugsy*, *The Long Day Closes*, and *Swoon*. Though none "lied," all pushed, pounded, and poeticized the facts till they turned to art. . . . Fidelity, whether to biographical truth or literary text, is a pedant's virtue.

Along with Andrews, most of the writers I spoke to in preparing this book also argued that truth was just the beginning. They acknowledged its force but, when push came to shove, argued that they were dramatists before they were reporters.

THE KEY QUESTIONS

Though the blurring of fact and fiction in dramadocs is a favorite topic of discussion among academics, I think there are only three issues at the heart of the matter that should trouble the writer:

Accuracy
Authorship and attitude
Audience, and social responsibility

Accuracy

You need to resolve for yourself from the start what level of authenticity and accuracy you are offering in regard to dialogue, characters, and events.

I've discussed dialogue elsewhere, but the issue is fairly simple. Where feasible, and when it is sufficiently dramatic, you try to retain authentic dialogue. Where that's not possible, and that's probably 90 percent of the time, you'll go on to create your own. As far as invented dialogue, not only does it have to be entertaining and compelling, but it should also be in keeping with the character being portrayed. Thus, the dialogue for McKellar, in *Public Enemies*, is invented but very close to what the congressman might have said.

Where you use real-life characters, you tend to aim for accuracy every time. Habits. Personality. Motivation. Traits. Modes of thought. Actions. All these things you usually want to make as close to the truth as possible.

You will also invent composite characters, or necessary characters. Sometimes, they will be based on real people, like Margaret Thatcher's hallucinatory husband in *The Iron Lady*, or the invented friend who accompanies the hero on his journey in *Malcolm X*. On rare occasions, as in *Skokie*, the invented person may even be your protagonist.

In films dealing with relatively contemporary events, you want, where feasible, to stay as close to the truth of the matter as you can. People want to know what really happened in the Birmingham pub bombings, the 9/11 tragedy, or on United 93—and your duty is to give them the information accurately and dramatically.

What people often fail to realize is that there is a difference between truth and accuracy. You can never give the whole truth. You are selecting events and characters to give a version of the truth, and *selecting* is the key word. Your aim, at least in contemporary news docudramas, is accuracy in everything you write about after you have made the selection, and that includes not just the facts, but also mood, atmosphere, and feeling.

Authorship and Attitude

We want something to be true, but whose truth are we talking about? Where do authorship and point of view come into the equation? The answer is right at the start.

Point of view and authorship may be negligible factors in the writing of a simplistic murderess-of-the-week docudrama, but they are vital considerations in writing about any complex issue or political film. What we have to acknowledge—and yet people seem very reluctant to do this—is that truth is very much in the eye of the beholder. If that's too strong, we can put it another way. Filmmakers may not lie, but they select facts for their films that fit in with their prejudices and their point of view on their subject.

JFK was made by Oliver Stone and offers a conspiracy theory about Kennedy's assassination. Few might agree, but Stone was free to have his day. *Gandhi* was made by a British filmmaker who totally admired his subject. To have expected the film to be a muckraking, warts-and-all portrayal is just nonsense. On the opposite side, one also suspects that *The Iron Lady* was written by someone not particularly enthusiastic about Margaret Thatcher's achievements.

Payments also cloud the issue. Both NBC and CBS made films about Amy Fisher, the girl from Long island who shot the wife of her lover, Joey Buttafuoco. One network had paid Amy for her story, the other had paid Joey for his. The points of view of the film were totally opposed. What's the moral? Sometimes, truth comes via the checkbook.

Audience

The easiest way for the scriptwriter to resolve the issue of truth may be simply to ask, "What does the *audience* expect? What level of accuracy does it want? Will my blend of fact and fiction confuse people, or will they be able to sort out one from the other?" My suspicion is that the audience's expectations vary with period, distance from the subject, the nature of the subject, and whether they are watching something on TV or in the cinema. William Goldman, the screenwriter of *All the President's Men*, once said that as far as movies are concerned, it is not important what is true; it is important what audiences accept as true. With the ability of the screenwriter to shape and twist the script, this is not a view I accept.

Period. If one looks at cinema audiences from, say, 1920 to 1950, one can well argue that their expectation of accuracy was minimal. I think they knew that when Hollywood touched history or biography, it was portraying an entertaining romance, rather than truth. When Sam Goldwyn said, "If you want to send a message, then use Western Union," he could well have added, "and if you want truth go to the history books, not Hollywood."

Hollywood was in the business of making money, and creating myths that sold. To do that, immense liberties were taken with truth and with facts. Poetic license, if one can call it that, ruled the day. Did it matter if Babe Ruth, Lou Gehrig, and Knute Rockne weren't quite the heroes they were painted to be? Not really. And what if a love interest was invented for George M. Cohan? So what if Hollywood covered up Cole Porter's homosexuality? Who cared? Certainly not the audience, who knew they were being treated to a fairy tale.

Today, audiences' expectations are different. I think they are still willing to a certain extent to go along with the fairy tale, but much less so. Conditioned by TV news and documentaries, and by a higher educational level, they want a greater degree of truth. Thus, the seamier side of politicians and the sexual affairs of our leaders are often shown in a spotlight that would have been unacceptable in the media a few years ago.

In 2003, the British Standards Commission published a study called *Dramatic License.* After examining the whole area of fact-based drama on TV, they came up with some surprising conclusions. The most interesting one was that the while the audience was willing to accept something less than the truth in contemporary docudrama, it was less willing to forgive inaccuracy in historical films. The reasoning seemed to be that while it was often difficult to establish basic facts regarding current events, they should be known in the case of past history. However, there was a slight softening in the executive summary of the report, which stated:

> Although entertainment is the most important factor for viewers, they still expect the story or situation to be based on fact. They expect a realistic portrayal with an element of factual accuracy, but viewers also accept that, for drama's sake, exaggeration of a situation or concentration on one possible outcome is needed to entertain.

Subject, Time, Distance. I also believe that the demand for accuracy varies with time distance from the subject. Historic romances are just that:

romances, and no more. Columbus peels an orange for his son and looks at the horizon, and we smile, and if he falls in love with Queen Isabella, good for him. But if you take too many liberties in contemporary subject matter, like *The Queen* or *Patton*, you may be asking for trouble.

And often, it must be said, the audience seems to prefer romance and fantasy in distant history to the truth. When Hollywood made *Mutiny on the Bounty*, in the 1930s, it was one of the most popular films of its day. But truth was rent apart. Thus, Captain William Bligh, a navigator of genius, and called by one historian "a humane and considerate commander," is portrayed as a sadistic tyrant. However, his second-in-command, Fletcher Christian, inexperienced and possibly unstable, is shown as the intrepid hero. History went down the drain, but profits soared. By way of contrast, the 1984 film *The Bounty*, with Anthony Hopkins playing Bligh, stayed much closer to the facts. This may have been its downfall. The audience was disappointed there was no sadistic swashbuckler here and simply stayed away.

The nature of the subject. After observing the failure of *The Bounty*, my guess is that audiences' expectation of truth and accuracy varies with the nature of the subject, and its importance in their daily lives. While we don't care that much why a murderess sets out on her life of crime, or a guy becomes a boxer like his brother, we do care about corruption in the White House, the lead-up to 9/11, oil spills, and the framing of Irish suspects for political murders. The greater our concern about the subject, the greater our need for truth.

Bearing this in mind, we can understand the concern some years ago over *Mississippi Burning* and *JFK*. Both films dealt with searing political issues affecting us to this day, that is, civil rights abuses and possible conspiracy in a political assassination. Both films lied, prevaricated, and invented spurious characters and questionable facts. *Mississippi Burning* created an FBI concern with the killing of civil rights workers that was totally at odds with fact, even crediting the discovery of the murdered bodies to the FBI. *JFK*, based on the questionable viewpoint of Jim Garrison, ignored the findings of the Warren Commission and proposed a highly dubious conspiracy theory.

The ground is strewn with similar films that have been flawed but have seriously affected our thinking. In the 1920s, the heroic sailors' demonstration of solidarity with the common people in *Battleship Potemkin* became an inspiration for the left in Europe. In fact, the sailors were not particularly interested in the fate of the people of Odessa, and the ship's guns, when they did fire, simply missed their target. Closer to our own time, the ABC TV series *Roots* portrayed slavery from the slaves' point of view. The abuse of the Africans rightly troubled the conscience of most of the viewers. It was just a pity that so much of the history was distorted. The complicity of African tribes in the enslavement of other tribes was totally ignored. Nor was the tribal home of Kunta Kinte exactly a blissful garden of Eden before the white man came.

Do these travesties matter? Yes, because these films have become the basis for the formation of the political attitudes of a new generation, for whom such films, and TV shows, are the main means of getting in touch with the past. When writers claim their films capture historic truth despite inaccuracies, then I sense that film and history part ways.

In regard to truth versus fiction, 2013 was a seminal year for bringing many of the controversies to the fore. Tony Kushner, for example, the screenwriter of *Lincoln*, was criticized for changing the historical record on the congressional vote for the Thirteenth Amendment. In his version, two representatives from Connecticut seemed to have approved slavery, which a few Democrats saw as a slight on history.

The gap between truth and creative license in *Zero Dark Thirty* was also criticized by both liberals and Republicans for its depiction of torture and waterboarding. The writers of *Argo* also drew comment for inventing facts such as a sequence where armed Iranian guards chase a departing American plane down the runway.

In a remark in the *New York Times*, Mark Boal, screenwriter of *Zero Dark Thirty*, is quoted as saying that *Lincoln*, *Argo*, and *Zero Dark Thirty* "work as business, with audiences, and with critics, and I don't know what more you could really ask for."[1] Well if those are your criteria, you certainly know what examples to follow. And, again, as in *Birth of a Nation*, we have to ask, are we watching history or propaganda? As a writer, I would try to avoid creating the latter.

SIGNPOSTING

If the audience has certain expectations of truth and accuracy, I believe it helps to let them know on what basis you've constructed the script.

This is a fairly radical idea, not practiced in Hollywood, but gaining favor in European television, and particularly in the field of journalistically and politically based docudramas. The English filmmaker Leslie Woodhead puts the challenge and the solution this way:

> I am convinced that the makers of dramatized documentary do have a special obligation to let the audience know what they are up to, what's been called by one American critic: "the right not to be deliberately mislead."
>
> In any one program, it's likely that the material being dramatized will be derived from a variety of sources of varying status. It seems to me vital to signpost material to avoid as far as possible a confusion in the audience about levels of credibility.

---

1. Mark Boal, *New York Times*, February 14, 2013, C2.

What Woodhead means by signposting is in fact a fairly simple process. It means telling the audience at the beginning of the film the basis for your filmic material. This usually means a short note saying that the central material comes from a smuggled tape of a crucial meeting, for instance, or that this film is based on the diaries of Katrin and Ivan, supplemented by conversations with them, and use of the court records.

Ignorance and conjecture are also indicated. So, close to the end of *The Tragedy of Flight 103*, we are clearly told by the producers of the film that the final details leading to the Pan Am crash are obscure. Having said that, they suggest that events are very likely to have progressed in a certain way. It's not as neat as going on without pause, but certainly more fair.

SUGGESTED BY . . .

Many times, writers take real situations and crises, write a drama around the events, and label the outcome "a dramatic presentation having no resemblance to real personalities and events." Does that help things? Does that help you evade responsibility for accuracy? Sometimes, we are not even offered that disclaimer. We are entering murky waters here. My response is to be very careful, because the audience will ignore your cover statement and accept your story as the *real* genuine article.

This happened in the Canadian TV series *The Boys of St. Vincent*, which was broadly based on a scandal at a Newfoundland orphanage run by the Irish Christian Brothers. The original saga was a revolting story of physical and sexual assault by pedophile men who ran the orphanage, and official indifference amounting to virtual complicity. A terrible story, but very interesting material for TV. The series came out with the usual labels of "no resemblance," but no one was fooled. The events on the screen very closely reflected what had occurred in Newfoundland, yet the disclaimers eschewed all responsibility for accuracy. With this disclaimer in hand, the producers intermingled fact and fiction more freely than usual, leaving an audience totally bewildered as to what was what. More seriously, the Christian Brothers could claim that what was represented was pure fiction.

The 2002 film *The Magdalene Sisters*, written by Peter Mullan, can be seen in a similar light. The film deals with four girls being sent to the Irish Catholic Magdalene Asylums (also known as the Magdalene laundries.) These were homes for girls and women who, for example, had become pregnant and were considered fallen by their families or society. In the film, their treatment is seen as cruel, harsh, and extremely sadistic. Though the film was offered as fiction, most people recognized it as a very accurate portrayal of past general conditions in the Magdalene laundries, some even saying the situation had been even worse than portrayed by Mullan. The asylums were closed in 1996, six years before the making of the film, but Mullan stated his reason for making the film was that the girls had received no apology, expressions of regret, or compensation.

"No resemblance" seems to me a term people use when they want deniability, but also want the audience to say, "yes, this is real." Other terms that fudge the issue are "loosely based on," "inspired by," and "true to the spirit of." Frankly, I never know quite what they mean, except that the writer and producer are usually taking a hell of a lot of liberties with the truth. They want to draw you in with the attraction of a real-life story, but at the same time want to have the freedom of fiction, but maybe you'll think otherwise when you start writing.

TRUE TO THE SPIRIT

When Hollywood made their dozens of biopics in the 1940s, they usually boasted about the work of their research departments. In reality, the boasting didn't have much to support it. The vaunted research had more to do with clothes and furniture than with investigating the true nature of the biopic's subject. Accuracy was just a pretended selling point, tolerated so long as it didn't get in the way of a strong emotional and dramatic story.

Biography presents a multitude of problems to the writer, not the least being that few lives are dramatic, and even when they are, they can be hell to translate into an interesting dramatic form.

When the great comic director Preston Sturges started writing a film on the life of Dr. William Morton, the discover of ether as an anesthetic, he ran into an immediate problem. Morton's discovery came early in his life, and then nothing else of interest happened. In short, the most dramatic event came in the first act. There was only one solution according to Sturges in his biography: alter the order of things.

> I believe a biographer has two obligations. He must be true to his subject and he must not bore his public. Since he cannot change the chronology of events he can only change the order of presentation. Dr. Morton's life, as lived was a very bad piece of dramatic construction. A few months of excitement and twenty years of boredom. . . . My job was to show a play about Dr. Morton's life. To have a play you must have a climax, and it's better not to have the climax right at the beginning.

The most interesting comment is in Sturges's second sentence; in other words, "Thou shalt not bore thy public." But he also suggests a second commandment. "Thou shalt be true to thy subject." Now that looks almost as easy as "Don't commit murder or adultery" yet is the writer's commandment which is most frequently broken.

But who determines what the true spirit is? Me, you, the voters for the Oscar? I grant there are difficulties yet would still argue that in most cases the public does have a common viewpoint on what constitutes the essential truth about a person, and the essence of his or her real persona.

How does all this affect you as a writer? It means that you have to remember that accuracy is only a beginning. Beyond that, you have to capture the real spirit of a person. If you fail in that, then—however technically accurate your film is in regard to facts, details, dates, and events—it will be a failure.

The danger usually starts with the canonization of the subject. The distortion is compounded by a failure to show anything really negative, or complex, or puzzling about the hero. As the blandness increases, the essence is removed from the character, and he or she gradually becomes everyman or everywoman, with a little bit of nobility added. Which makes for wonderful statues and lousy films.

This happened in *Gandhi*, *Malcolm X*, and *Chaplin*. In the first two, instead of being presented by real people we were presented with saints. Terence Rafferty expressed it best in the *New Yorker* when he wrote, "*Malcolm X* is stubbornly impersonal. It has a sort of high-school field-trip quality, an explicitly educational tone. It's revelatory, but dull." The crime is clear: Malcolm was robbed of his individuality.

Again, David Attenborough's *Chaplin* bears hardly any resemblance to the genius, sharp businessman, and woolly leftist the world knew. This time, we can't blame a scriptwriter, because there were four.

Little is shown of the women in Charlie's private life. Little time is spent showing how Charlie worked as an artist. Instead, we have a film-by-numbers saga about a morose Englishman that is totally impersonal, and totally fails to evoke anything of Chaplin's magnetism or drive.

Yet there is hope. In recent years, writers (and producers) have tended to show the warts and failings of our heroes much more realistically than in the past. We see that Marilyn Monroe can be a pain in the neck; that the Queen of England isn't perfect; that Mark Zuckerberg can be quite a schemer; that one wouldn't necessarily want to spend time with Truman Capote; and that even Harvey Milk has his problems. Of course, all their films have faults, and occasionally dip into the barrel of clichés. But they are also dynamic, vivid, and pulsating. The heroes we see are real and believable.

In the end, such biographical films, including those about Stalin, Margaret Thatcher, President Nixon, and others, fulfill Sturges's two commandments. They are rarely boring, and they are true to their subjects. They catch the man or the woman behind the myth, and that is all one can ask.

12. Rights and Legal Issues

Before I became a filmmaker, I worked as a film attorney in London. Every day, writers and producers came to our office in hope and in fear. Their stories were usually similar. They had landed a movie deal but wanted to make sure it was airtight. They wanted to make sure they would get promised money on time, that they wouldn't be sued for what they were doing, that they could go ahead in peace, and that the project didn't have any dangers.

They were all creative people and had the sense to realize that they needed legal advice, not just to protect their rights and percentages, and to ensure their fees, but also to protect themselves against damaging court actions.

In this chapter, I'll try to give you a simplified overview of the chief professional and legal issues you are likely to encounter as a writer of docudrama. I hope this will help you see where the problems are. How do you cope with them? Only one answer makes sense. You get yourself a good lawyer. Fact-based films can be dangerous territory, and only a competent attorney can safeguard your rights, and provide you with some legal advice you might need on the journey.

Though you'll find many legal questions continually dropping on your head, you have only a few main concerns:

Your script rights
Contractual relations with your producer
Books and copyrights
Rights of your film subject
The demands of the networks

YOUR SCRIPT RIGHTS

You've finished an original script and your friends think it's terrific. You're itching to send it off to a producer or a network, but the first thing you have to do is protect your copyright—and get a public record of authorship to ensure that the script doesn't get plagiarized. You can do this in one of three ways.

First, any writer, whether a member of the Writers Guild of America or not, can register his or her treatment, complete script, or outline of a fully developed unique story with the guild. But you cannot register ideas, so be careful to whom you speak when discussing your project. The fees for registration at the moment of writing are $10 for guild members, $25 for nonmembers, and they give you protection from five to ten years.

On receipt of your script, the guild will put it on microfilm and store it in safety. If your script is later plagiarized, the guild's custodian of records can be summoned to appear on your behalf. Particulars of the registration procedure can be obtained from the registration office: Writers Guild of America, 7000 West Third St., Los Angeles, CA 90048, or 250 Hudson St., New York, NY, 10013.

Second, you can take out a formal *copyright.* This is done by registering your script with the U.S. Copyright Office. The cost is $45, and you can get the forms online. However, you should note it can take up to six months to get official recognition. The cost is slightly more than registering with the Writers Guild but gives you longer protection. Also on the plus side, your ability to obtain legal fees and damages, if your script has been plagiarized, is slightly better using the copyright office.

Third, the simplest way of all to protect your material is to seal it in an envelope, and send it to yourself, special delivery. It is vital that the postmark can be clearly seen, as that's the main proof of date of authorship. Whatever you do, you must not open the envelope, or your efforts will have been for nothing. This method of safeguarding your work is sometimes called "the poor man's copyright." It seems to save money but has a serious drawback. It has been known for the postmarks and special delivery to be faked, and a good lawyer might well question the validity of this copyright method in court.

CONTRACTUAL RELATIONS WITH YOUR PRODUCER

The possible markets for your scripts include independent producers, production companies like Lionsgate, the major studios, the networks, and television offshoots like Film Four. If they like your work, they may option it, buy it outright, or take you on as a writer for hire and get you to work on their own pet projects.

Your task, therefore, is really twofold. You have to get your work read and tentatively accepted. Once that's been accomplished, you have to get yourself the best deal possible.

Submission

Agents. Most writers submit their work through an agent. If a sale is made, the agent will take a percentage of your fee as his or her commission. The advantage of a good agent is that he is familiar with the market, knows best where to send your script, and, if he believes in it, will really push your work.

If he has been around a few years, he will probably have a good relationship and track record with a large number of producers. This means his recommendations will be taken seriously.

If your script is accepted for a sale or option, or if the producer wants generally to hire you as a writer, your agent will help you negotiate terms.

Can you exist without an agent? Yes! But it's not advisable. Every serious writer that I know works through an agent. Occasionally, a writer may make an independent submission to a producer, or pitch an idea without the help of an agent, but usually the agent is there as advisor and facilitator.

The problem is that it can be quite hard for an unproven writer to get an agent. This means you may have to submit your script directly to the producer or network, without an intermediary. There are two drawbacks to this.

The first is that because producers are overwhelmed with scripts, and don't know you, your script may finish up in the garbage can, unread. As maybe twenty to thirty thousand scripts bounce around Hollywood and New York every year, you can possibly understand the producers' dilemmas. So just getting your script seen can be a major hurdle, and dozens of books have been written offering both practical and esoteric advice on overcoming this obstacle.

The second point is that producers dislike plagiarism suits. They are afraid that if they reject your script and later make a film on a similar theme, you may attack them in court for copying your work. Thus, the easiest escape for them is to return your work, unopened. This point doesn't arise when the script is submitted through a recognized agent. The afterword of this book contains discussion of how to get an agent.

Waivers. One way producers get out of this dilemma is to ask for a release form—a waiver—in advance of opening your script. The form states that the company has no obligation to you, and that you waive any right to sue if the company produces a similar work.

This demand for a waiver is now standard in most production and television companies. However, very often one waiver will cover you not just in the present case, but for all future work as well that you submit to the company.

Where to submit. If you have written a feature film, your script is a candidate for production everywhere except the networks, and even there one finds exceptions. Film Four in England (a branch of Channel 4), for example, has for years encouraged and partially financed films like *127 Hours*, *Touching the Void*, and *Slumdog Millionaire*.

In American television, your best bet for the placement of scripts is with good independent producers like Martin Poll, Buzz Berger, Lionsgate, and Rosemont Productions, to name just a few.

What you are looking for is a producer who has already made one or two docudramas, and has good access to the networks. You go to these people because they can move your script forward in a way that you probably can't. They know the ropes, have a reputation and a track record, and can get the project considered seriously at the broadcast level.

You can approach the commercial networks directly, but it is doubtful if you'll get a proper hearing. They mainly act as financial sponsors, rather than as actual producers, and usually negotiate with and listen to only known production companies.

Things are slightly different in England and maybe a fraction looser. There, it is more acceptable to approach Channel 4 or the drama section of the BBC directly with your script or idea. But, again, it's preferable to go through a known production company.

The Deal

If a producer likes your work, he or she may suggest purchasing your work outright, optioning it, or taking you on as a writer for hire. Whichever happens, you've got a tentative *deal*, or basic agreement. The terms have to be negotiated and can be tricky, and this is where you might call in your agent or your lawyer.

After your first basic discussions, a deal memo is drawn up, outlining the main points of the agreement, and covering fees, rights, royalties, credits, and a dozen other points. A formal *contract* is then drawn up, based on the memo but defining every little detail. As most American producers are signatories to an agreement with the Writers Guild (and you'll probably be a member by this time), the contract will follow and maybe enlarge on the minimum basic agreement terms laid down by the guild.

If you have sold your script outright, you may be paid in full immediately, or be asked to delay part of the payment until the start of shooting. This is fine so long as payment is not dependent on shooting, and a date is fixed for payment if shooting is delayed. If someone suggests part payment, with more to come if and when they commence the film, you are not really talking of an outright sale but have moved into the area of options.

The Option

We've talked about options before in regard to your purchasing a book or trying to buy the rights to someone's life story. In negotiating with a producer, the roles are reversed. The producer wants an option from you on your script, so that, in turn, he can see if he can do what he needs to do to get the production off the ground. Regarding a television movie, the producer is taking an option to see whether he can get a network or a major cable company interested in the project.

The option is exclusive and gives the producer the right to hunt around for a specific length of time, often six months on a TV project and a year on a film. The option sum can be quite small, say $3,000 or $4,000, but a much larger sum is paid if the script is sold, that is, if the option is taken up.

This purchase price for the rights is fixed when the option is drawn up, and the initial payment becomes part of it. Thus if the final sum is $60,000 and the option $5,000, only $55,000 will be paid if the script is bought. If the option is renewed for a further six months for another $5,000, this second sum does *not* become part of the final payment. If the option is not taken up at the end of the defined period, all the script rights remain with you.

The Step Deal

If a producer has been introduced to your work and likes it, he or she may ask you to develop new material or write a script for a project he or she has in hand. The agreement that covers your relationship is called the *step deal* and usually follows the standard Writers Guild contract for freelance writers. The term *step deal* comes from the fact that the obligations and payments are set out in stages. Only when each stage is complete do you move on to the next one.

If your project is to adapt a book, your first task will be to prepare a treatment. The payment for this is usually 30 percent of the overall agreed sum. If the treatment is accepted, you will usually be asked to go on and do the *first draft*, though the producer has the right to assign this to someone else. When you deliver the draft, you will be paid another 40 percent of the fee. The final option of the producer is to ask you or someone else to do the final draft. Once that's turned in, you get the balance of your fee.

As you can see, the step deal is set out to safeguard the producer at every stage. He is the one who has the option to continue or break off the relationship. On your side, you are guaranteed payment at fixed stages, whether or not the producer gets to the starting line.

Besides payments, the contract will also specify delivery dates and credits. As most producers are also signatories to agreements with the Writers Guild, the contract will also ask you to become or remain a member of the guild. If you are not already a member, the existence of your agreement with the producer will enable you to join.

The above sets out the basic lines of agreement, but they will vary slightly according to the situation. Sometimes, you will work up a story, or do a revised treatment. At other times, you may be asked to do a polish of someone else's material, or do a rewrite beyond the second draft. Each of these points has to be incorporated into the contract.

It is important to note that the Writer's Guild sets out minimum fees for different parts of the writing task, and you should write to the guild to see what these are. You'll see the fees differ between theatrical projects and TV dramas. Thus, for theatrical films it sets out scales for story, first draft, second draft, rewrites, and polishes. The scale also differs between low-budget and high-budget films. Payment for TV network films are lower than for cinema projects, and it is split between sums for story and teleplay, and for add-on sums for rewrites. The amount agreed on also differs according to the length of the movie.

Television

The biggest market for docudrama, or at least biopics, is television, and as mentioned above, the minimum rate for your script is fixed by agreements between the producers, the networks, and the Writers Guild. Guild membership is open to anyone who has had a writers contract with a producer recognized by the guild.

Though the guild sets out minimum fees, what you actually receive depends on your negotiating power. For example, both Paul Monash and Larry Gelbart (both now unfortunately deceased) were top feature writers. When the one wrote *Stalin* and the other *Barbarians at the Gates*, their fees were reputed to be quite astronomical, and light-years removed from the guild minimums.

Obviously, fame and a track record help in boosting your dollars, but since the fee-negotiating process is an open one, I would always argue for using a good agent. With help, even as a beginner, you may be able to raise the selling price of your script or of your general work.

Feature Films

Feature films offer the cream, and many writers see television work as inferior. However, one has to face certain facts. While the fees for features can be astronomical, there is also far less work around. Once again, minimum fees are fixed by the guild, but the actual sums paid may bear no relation to guild scales.

Generally, the fees paid for a feature are in direct relation to the scale of the budget, with fees of one to two million dollars becoming fairly common for super productions like *The Lord of the Rings* or *Avatar*. Fees for fact-based films like *The King's Speech* or *The Fighter* haven't quite reached these heights, but have still been quite substantial, into six or sometimes low seven figures.

Will you be able to command a high fee? In the beginning, however good your script, the answer is probably "no." But Hollywood is a strange town. All you need is one big hit, or one or two solid successes, and the sky's your limit.

BOOKS AND COPYRIGHTS

When you are considering adapting either a book or a play for a script, both the option and full purchase of the rights have to be set out in a formal contract. The option will contain almost exactly the same clauses as the purchase of rights, except that it sets the purchase in the future, and the purchase is subject to certain conditions. Below I've set out the main subjects you'll see mentioned in most options and purchase contacts.

Option Fee and Purchase Price

There is no standard fee for purchasing an option. Sometimes, you may get an option for nothing. Sometimes, it might be as low as $500 or as high as $70,000. Everything depends on who wants the rights, competition for them, how long they've been around, and your bargaining power.

If the book is a best seller—like *Steve Jobs*, by Walter Isaacson, or *The Accidental Billionaires*, by Ben Mezrich, about Mark Zuckerberg—you will definitely have to pay top dollar for an option, if you can get it at all. In many cases, the book is so popular the author does not want to waste time on the uncertainties of options, and will be interested only in an outright sale, which could well reach $300,000 to a million dollars for a best seller.

The competition will also be a factor in figuring out both the option and final purchase price. The more competitors, the stiffer the price. This is one reason producers like to try to get hold of books while they are still in the manuscript or proof stage. They want to see the story's worth while the book is unknown, its value unassessed, and competition for it minimal. The downside of this action is that the book can turn out to be a failure, but taking an early option to beat the competition may be worth the chance.

The fixing of the final price when you option a play or a book is exactly the same as when a producer options your own script. You fix the price when you take out the option, and that's the price that becomes payable if you take up the option. As mentioned before, your first option payment becomes part of the final purchase price.

Sometimes, you can get depressed reading about astronomical sums being paid for book rights. You say to yourself, "How can I ever compete in such a realm?" Maybe you can't. But if you look around, you'll find there are a tremendous number of books that have been neglected, or were once popular and now forgotten, that could make great docudramas. In these cases, you may well be able to purchase an option for a relatively low sum. The biography of Sir Richard Burton, the explorer, not the actor, is a case in point.

Born in the early nineteenth century, Burton was soldier, adventurer, Arabist, and one of the greatest linguists of his age. He was one of the first white men to enter the forbidden city of Mecca, and his search for the source of the Nile with John Hanning Speke forms the basis for William Harrison's novel *Mountains of the Moon*. The book came out in 1982 and was filmed a decade later by Bob Rafelson.

The producers probably paid a chunk of money for the book rights. One is left to wonder whether they had heard of *Burton: A Biography*, written by Byron Farwell and published without fanfare in 1963. My guess is that an option on Farwell's book, which is much more interesting than Harrison's, could have been purchased for a song had one been wise enough at the time.

Sometimes, the lawyers for the original author may suggest the insertion of a clause awarding their client not just payment for the book rights, but also a percentage of any net profits you, the scriptwriter, or the producer make on the film. Be careful of such a clause. It can lead to great complications and should never be inserted without the advice of your lawyer.

Length of the Option

Your option has to cover a long enough period for you to get the project off the ground. This can mean first writing a proposal based on the book; then writing a treatment or full script; and then offering your work to a production company or network for fuller development. All this can take months or years.

If you are a beginner, or a writer without screen credits, the owner of the rights may want to limit your option to six months. However, the usual period for an option is at least a year, with a right to renew it for further payment. Eyebrows get raised if the option goes on for too long, but I have seen options renewed for three or four years as the would-be screenwriter has plugged away, trying to find a buyer for his or her script.

Whether you go for a short-term or long-term option, it must be exclusive. Without exclusivity, you may find you've done a great deal of work, but someone else has got the film going before you. To avoid such a scenario, you have to obtain exclusivity.

Locating the Rights

Before you can option anything, you have to find out who has the rights, which is usually a fairly simple process.

To trace the rights to a book, you simply write to the publisher or the author's agent. In turn, they will tell you who owns the rights, whether it's the publisher or the author, or maybe someone else altogether to whom the rights have been assigned. Sometimes, an author may have died, and his executors control the rights. Here, again, the publisher should be able to tell you whom to contact.

Occasionally, a biographical play comes up, like *Frost/Nixon*, and here too there are various approaches. First, you may be able to find the address of the playwright or his agent from the Writers Guild. If the play is in print, it has most likely been published by either Samuel French or the Dramatists Play Service, both of whom are located in New York. Both bodies will be able to help you locate the owner of the rights.

If an exclusive story appears in a magazine, such as an exposé on banks, or on drugs, your first move is to contact the magazine. They will either own the rights or put you in touch with the author.

Public Domain and Expired Copyright

If the material you are hunting for is in the public domain, you won't have to go through the hassle of obtaining rights, as the use of the material is open to everyone. Public domain covers two broad sections of written materials—expired copyright, and materials that are part of the public record.

As copyright rules vary from country to country, you have to be very careful what rules apply. In the U.S., copyright statutes basically protect a book or an article written after 1978 for seventy years after the death of the author, or for ninety-five years if it was a work written for hire. Anything written before 1927 is deemed out of copyright. In the U.K., the law is fairly similar, giving copyright protection for seventy years from the death of the author.

The second area of public domain covers all materials taken from public records, public agencies, media news stories, and court papers. What this means is that you can use all open official records, and all openly available information touching on someone who is in the public eye, though, as you'll see later, you still have to be careful about defamation.

In general, this has all made life a bit simpler for writers of docudrama. Although they were supplemented by various biographies, films like *Downfall*, about Hitler's last ten days, *The Iron Lady*, *Stalin*, and *Gandhi* were all mainly written from public domain materials.

A special treasure trove for you in public domain is the record of criminal trials. I used these extensively when writing *The First Fagin*, and they've provided inspiration for an amazing number of movies of the week, such as *Oppenheimer*, *Who Bombed Birmingham?*, *Willing to Kill*, *The Aileen Wuormos Story*, and *A Woman Scorned*, to name only a few.

Facts belong to everyone, and as a writer you can use them freely, so long as they are discoverable through the public domain. This means you can freely use the knowledge discovered from newspaper and TV stories but can't use facts that are only found in unpublished private letters. What should also be obvious, but is worth repeating, is that the appearance of a story in a newspaper is no guarantee of its truth.

RIGHTS OF YOUR FILM SUBJECT

When you want to write a script about someone's life and the material exists outside of a book, you have to ask a few basic questions. Is the material known, of public interest, and in the public domain, or will you have to purchase the rights to the story? Sometimes, even if the material is public, you ask yourself an extra question. Should I purchase the rights to their story from the people concerned, just to be safe?

The reason that producers don't just go ahead and purchase the rights is mainly financial. The purchase of various characters' rights in the famous Texas cheerleading murder story came to over $100,000, and the figure is likely to escalate. Not every writer or producer has that kind of money to play around with, so a close examination of material in the public domain becomes the first priority.

Whatever the source of material for your film, either you or your producer will have to consider several legal and practical questions before you can go ahead, including:

> Is the story potentially libelous?
> Will your film lay you open to a suit for invasion of privacy, or one of the other developing torts dealing with personal property rights?
> Is the story of sufficient public interest and notoriety that you can claim that an accurate depiction of it is allowable as use of known material in the public domain?
> Will you be allowed a certain license to write what you want under the protections of the First Amendment, regarding freedom of speech?

A lot of the answers vary with the facts, and with different state jurisdictions and rulings. You will find it hard to get definitive answers because the whole legal area is in a state of flux.

Defamation

Producers and networks run scared in the face of defamation threats and lawsuits. Defamation is generally defined as information likely to cause harm to a plaintiff's reputation in the eyes of the world. Usually it's split into two sections: slander, which is seen as defamation by speech, and libel, which is defamation by the printed word. Defamation in films is usually looked upon as libel. Definitions vary from state to state and country to country, as do defenses available. In some countries, truth of an allegation is a defense. In others, the prosecution has to prove malice. Although docudrama seems very open to accusations of defamation, very few people or organizations have brought court cases against writers and producers. This is due variously to the expense of bringing suit, to the fact that so many docudramas have been extensively researched, and to the defenses available, such as justification, fair comment, and privilege.

Nevertheless, most producers employ specialist lawyers (sometimes called "the thought police") to vet their scripts for defamation. Many times, the lawyers are overzealous, demanding written backup for many things said by the principals in the docudrama. This practice, incidentally, is also often demanded by the networks. However, one of the advantages of having lawyers vet the script is that it becomes easier to obtain the important E and O (errors and omissions) insurance coverage for the production.

Public Personalities and the Right of Privacy

Stories of public figures, including entertainers, politicians, and high-profile businessmen, provide the lifeblood of docudramas. So hardly a month goes by without Marilyn Monroe, the Kennedys, President Bush, Peter Sellers, Tina Turner, Margaret Thatcher, the queen of England, Bill Gates, or Mark Zuckerberg turning up in a feature or on the TV screen.

The general rule for public figures like politicians and media celebrities is that they are considered to have given up much of their right to privacy. This means, broadly speaking, that one can write about them with a greater freedom than in the case of a private person, though you still have to be careful as regards defamation.

But what about privacy and the private individual. Does he or she have a right to privacy? On certain matters like health, and finances, the general answer is "yes," but otherwise the case is not so clear. In England, for example, one cannot bring an action for invasion of privacy, and in the U.S. the right of privacy is not guaranteed under the Constitution.

The right of privacy is sometimes referred to as the "right to be left alone." If a person thinks his or her privacy has been invaded, he or she may be able to bring a civil action for damages. The tort is a developing one, not often pursued because of its lack of certainty and case backing, but at the moment seems to cover four areas:

Intrusion on someone's seclusion or solitude
Public disclosure of embarrassing facts
Publicity which places a person in a false light in the public eye
Appropriation, for the defendant's advantage, of the plaintiff's name or likeness

Translated into ordinary language, this means that if your script is offensive, or if you knew parts of it were false, or if you recklessly disregarded this possibility, you could possibly be sued. The defense may be that the story was accurate, newsworthy, in the public domain, and inoffensive. You can also plead the First Amendment, the right of freedom of speech.

In practice, and following the First Amendment, the courts have tended to move against restricting the freedoms of a writer, at least in docudrama. For example, they've allowed dramatic tricks like "telescoping" to move events along, and they've allowed a great deal of leeway in reconstructing conversations. When debating the merit of a script, they also tend to give more consideration to the public's right to be informed than to the individual's right to privacy.

In practice, though the right to privacy is frequently discussed, very few privacy claims have been decided outside of defamation. This means there are few guidelines as to the extent to which a person's life story can really be used without his or her permission.

The Right of Publicity

Although the right to publicity may be difficult to prove, lawyers have recently been developing another personal right, the right to publicity. What the courts seem to be saying here is that a person's name, reputation, and life story make up an economic asset, a saleable commodity, and a potential commercial property right. Once having recognized this, the corollary is that only the subject in question can control the commercial exploitation of his or her life.

While the law has been used to protect unauthorized pictures of certain actors' faces on billboards, or imitation of their voices for adverts, it's not clear how this can or will affect docudrama. But, again, beware of what's happening.

Optioning a Life Story

After a number of years of writing docudramas and documentaries, I feel that where feasible, you should always try to take an option on a private individual's life story. There are good reasons for this. When you take material from the public domain, you lay yourself open to possible actions for defamation, for invasion of privacy, and for stealing publicity rights. As I've argued above, in most situations the plaintiff will find it very hard to prove his case, but that's almost irrelevant.

The reality is that once an action starts, the hassles, the legal proceedings, and the threats of injunctions become more bother than they are worth. If you can avoid all possible lawsuit threats for the expenditure of a few thousand dollars, it seems to me well worth it.

There are a large number of benefits for signing an agreement with your subject, but the main ones are these:

> You can obtain a release against defamation, invasion of privacy, or exploitation of the life story rights.
> You can get the cooperation of the subject, and gain access to all sorts of private information that would have been impossible otherwise. You get "the inside story," which of course is the one everyone wants to hear.
> You are usually given the leeway to fictionalize.
> If you are lucky, you eliminate competition for the story.

You may find that in order to tell your story properly, or safeguard against competition, you may have to option more than one person's story. This can mean turning to relatives and friends as well as your main subject. So in the famous HBO film *The Positively Amazing True Adventures of the Alleged Texas Cheerleading Murdering Mom*, rights were purchased from almost all members of the two opposing families.

The contract that should be drawn up by a good lawyer is very similar to the option contract for a book. Once more, you will be paying attention to purchase price and the duration of the contract, and making sure it's exclusive. The contract will also make sure you are protected against legal suits from the subject.

One of the most important sections concerns exactly what rights are granted to you or the producer. Normally, the clause will state that, inter alia, you have the right "to depict the subject factually or *fictionally*, and to use the subject's name, likeness, voice, and biography in any and all media, and in all advertising and exploitation." In brief, you are going for complete control of the story and its use.

As in book contracts, you may want to provide for the subject to consult with you on the film. The fee for this should be fixed, and once again, all decisions about the script should be exclusively yours or the producer's.

THE DEMANDS OF THE NETWORKS

The main market for docudramas was once television, though that could be changing. When you or your producer submit a script or an idea to one of the TV networks or cable stations, it first goes to the programming department, or to the department specializing in your type of story. Thus HBO runs a docudrama unit, which would be the first to vet an idea or consider a script. Once a project has been given a tentative green light, it has to be approved by three departments.

The first of these is the legal department, which will check the option or purchase agreement to see that you've obtained all the necessary rights for making the film. The errors and omissions section then reviews the script to consider matters like defamation and possible invasion of privacy. Their job is to see that nothing appears or is shown that is likely to lead to a lawsuit. Finally, the script has to be reviewed by the broadcast standards and practices department, which examines the script minutely with regard to truth, fictionalization, and the way people are shown in the film.

Besides the general FCC rules warning about profanity, obscenity, and indecency, all the American networks have codified guidelines for the writing of fact-based films. ABC, for instance, asks that a person's known behavior patterns and attitudes be followed, while CBS warns its producers against materially altering or distorting the public record.

Though the details differ from network to network, they all essentially ask the producer and the writer the same thing. They want you to document the sources for the depiction of people in the script, whether books, articles, interviews, or anything else, and to indicate what is fact and what is fiction. To help you see this in more detail, I've reproduced the NBC guidelines in appendix A.

Few English stations or companies issue official guidelines, yet in practice they follow the same quest for authenticity and legal safeguards. Michael Eaton, the writer of *The Tragedy of Flight 103*, put it to me this way:

> Throughout the whole process of composition I am in constant contact with lawyers acting on behalf of the TV company making the film. I'm sending them drafts. I'm sending them scenes. And in those scenes I am giving them my sources and informing them what lines of dialogue are taken as verbatim record, and which ones I am inventing on the basis of various sources. In return the lawyers are informing me of what I can and can't do. And one of the things that can be quite frustrating to the dramatist is that if there is a difference of opinion between the lawyers and the dramatist, then I'm afraid it's the dramatist who loses the argument all the time.

One of the reasons for the guidelines and the close vetting of the scripts is that, as I have mentioned, it makes insurance of the programs much easier.

All networks, and any producers in their right mind, take out errors and omissions (E and O) insurance. This insurance covers the station and the network against all civil liabilities I mentioned earlier, like defamation. This means that if the network is sued, the E and O insurance covers the costs of the litigation. However, when the network applies for the insurance, it has to disclose all the facts about the script. It has to say whether it was done with permission, whether it was done with public domain materials, and what is fact and what is fiction. Because of all the earlier work, the answers to all these questions can then simply be found in the guideline response file, or in the scriptwriter's replies to the company lawyers.

FREEDOM FROM WORRY

By now, you are probably saying to yourself, "So many problems! Maybe I should become a lawyer instead of a writer." Well, perish the thought. You'll work harder and longer for much less personal satisfaction. I know. I've been there.

Docudrama does involve quite a lot of legalities, but apart from defamation and fictionalization, most of them are things you have to know about in principle rather than deal with in detail. Your attitude should be that of the director to the camera. A good director knows all about lenses but leaves the framing and the lighting to his director of photography. In the same way, you should be knowledgeable about the main legal problems behind writing docudrama but leave the day-to-day details to your agent or lawyer. This way you can get on with your main purpose, which is writing the great script.

AFTERWORD

You've finished. The bound script lies on your table in all its pristine glory. Next to it is a glass of wine. For once, your wastepaper basket is empty. The title in the middle of the first page says *To the Penal Colony*. Directly underneath it are the words "A screenplay by Irwin Nailer." In the lower right-hand corner of the page you've put your address and phone number. You feel proud. Exhausted. But what do you do next?

My own method is to have a gin and tonic, put the script aside for a few days, see a good film, and generally knock off for a while. Then after about a week, I look at it again and give it to a few friends to read, whose criticism I trust.

When I read it this time, I am trying to read it as an outsider. I look for flaws, problems, inconsistencies. I look at ways to improve the dialogue, which I now see is clunky in places. I tighten up the scenes, increase the tension, and overall try to make the drama work even better. I also listen very carefully to my friends' comments. Some I reject, but those that seem reasonable I try to incorporate into the script.

What I am trying to do is make the script as good as possible before I send it out, because I know I have only one chance with each producer who reads it.

AGENTS

The best way of getting your script read is to have it submitted to a producer by a good agent. Finding one can be as difficult as getting a good cup of coffee in the Sahara in the middle of a drought.

If you contact the Writers Guild of America, East or West, they will send you a list of agents who are signatories to the artists-managers agreement. This means they are authorized agents, and producers are willing to read unsolicited material from new writers if it comes through them. The ones who are open to new talent are marked with an asterisk on the guild's list. Under the guild's rules, an agency cannot contract with a writer for more than two years at a time; neither can its commission exceed 10 percent.

However, getting your script read by an agency, and signing a contract with it, are two different things. But at least the guild's list provides a first-attempt plan. Apart from working from the list, you use whatever friends and contacts you have to get yourself an agent. This is a process full of many letdowns and disappointments. Nevertheless, once you have a decent agent, you'll find that your script is given much greater consideration than if it were submitted out of the blue by yourself as a lone-star writer.

SCRIPT SUBMISSION

How you present your script to a would-be agent is of vital importance. It must make a terrific and professional first impression. It should be bound, clean, and made up of fresh A4 sized pages. Sounds obvious doesn't it? Yet many scripts are turned in stained and dog eared, as if proof of the burning of the midnight oil. Well, that's the road to immediate rejection and disaster.

Generally, the script should stand by itself. It should *not* be accompanied by masses of pages of explanation. However, two things are now acceptable after the first page title. If you want you can put in a *log line*. This is a dynamic one- or two-sentence explanation of the film. You can also provide a three- or four-paragraph synopsis of the film. As I say, these are possibilities, not prerequisites. Also feel free to send your script to as many agents as you like at the same time. No rule says you have to send the script out to only one agent at a time.

LOCALE

While there are a few writers who work best far from the madding crowd, this is not really possible for you as a beginning TV or feature scriptwriter. You must be at the heart of the action, which usually means New York or Los Angeles, or London or Manchester, or Sydney or Melbourne. The rationale is simple. You have to be around to talk, to consult, to talk, to modify, to badger, to schmooze, and to pitch—and to rewrite. And you can't do that from the heart of Tennessee or from the wilds of the Scottish highlands, unless your name is David Mamet and your fame is assured.

As a starting writer you have to be at a place where you can push, and push hard, at a moment's notice, so that you can extend your chances and grab whatever is available.

This leads to the crux of the matter. In practice, few writers manage to sell their first script easily, but it happens. Your script may be timely and extremely topical and may have arrived with the agent at just the right moment. But if your script is read, and then rejected, it offers an entry point.

It shows an agent or a producer that you can write. Thus, they may ask to see any of your future work. Or, seeing talent, they may want to take you on as a writer for hire. Thus your worth, so to speak, is proven on the job.

BREAKTHROUGHS

Rejection is probably harder for a writer than for an actor or director. Turned down one day, an actor can audition for a different part the following day. And if a director fails to get chosen for one film, there's always the chance something will come up the following week. In contrast, a writer may have put months of work in to a script, so that rejection may mean that a tremendous effort over time has simply gone down the drain.

This is the nature of the game, and it is to for everybody who plays it. For example, most studios maintain an alphabetical list of writers. Next to each writer's name is a list of his or her scripts that have been made into movies, and also a list of those that haven't. Even for a Hollywood winner like Joe Eszterhas, that second list of works shows eighteen unproduced screenplays. But the studio's list of writers also shows the names of those who came from nowhere and succeeded in breaking in, like Spike Lee and John Singleton. So there is hope.

Today, as I mentioned at the beginning of the book, the demand for docudrama is increasing, and I would almost call it a growth industry. The opportunities for writers are enormous, and though it may be hard at the beginning, if you are any good, you have to believe the breakthrough will come sooner rather than later. The breakthrough may take six months, it may take a year, but it will come.

SATISFACTIONS

When I started doing the research interviews for this book, besides asking the various writers about their techniques, I also asked them why they wrote, and what gave them the most satisfaction. All the writers were successful, some earning $200,000 to $300,000 a year from their scripts, and I expected them to put an emphasis on the financial rewards.

In fact, few did. Obviously, they liked the compensation, but to emphasize that was to miss the point.

Each said he liked to be his own man. They liked the isolation. They liked to be able to set their own hours, to work when they pleased, to knock off when they pleased. All of them said they responded to pressure, that it got the adrenalin running, that it focused them, and whipped up their creative drive.

A few came from a background of concerned documentary filmmaking. These were the ones who told me that what they liked about docudrama was the ability to break free of the limitations of documentary, and yet still aim to change the world.

What they all shared, however, was the sheer pleasure of sitting at the computer and knowing that through words they were going to build a world and a universe that would inspirationally be theirs alone. Others would people that universe, give it shape, form, color, and reality; but without the writers' words, there would have been silence. That, above all, was the greatest joy.

APPENDIXES

INDEX

Appendix A: Broadcast Guidelines

As mentioned earlier, all the U.S. networks have established guidelines for the writing of docudramas, or, as they like to call them, fact-based movies. These guidelines are issued by the networks' broadcast standards and practices departments. Each network has slightly different procedures, and below you can see the notes issued by NBC, along with the company's advice to producers.

NBC Guidelines

(Production Company name)
(Address)
(Re: (Name of the Project)

Dear _____

I am writing to advise you of the procedures that NBC requires producers and their attorneys to follow with respect to fact-based movies and mini-series. Production Company ("Packager") must do the following in connection with (Name of the Project):

1. Packager must obtain a completely annotated screenplay from the writer, with the annotations showing, line by line, whether particular dialogue is factual and accurate, fictionalized but based on known facts, or wholly author-created. Each notation should be keyed to underlying factual works, such as specific pages of newspaper articles, books, interviews, and the like. The more sensitive the particular scene or statement, the more important it is that there is substantial backup, including multiple sources. Please send one copy of the annotated script to the NBC Program Standards Department and a second copy to the NBC Law Department.

2. NBC expects Packager to be thoroughly familiar with all the events and occurrences that are reflected in the teleplay so that it can determine if particular sources upon which the author relies are sound or are contradicted by other sources.

Packager's attorneys will need to verify that the source chosen by the author is valid and supportable.

3. Because fact-based programs reflect real events, fictionalized material must be used only to advance the plot, not to alter what actually occurred. Therefore any author-created material must be carefully prepared to avoid placing an individual in a worse light than is completely supported by the facts.

4. The writer must take particular care with composite or fictional characters to ensure that there is no basis for a claim of accidental identification. In particular, the reviewing attorneys should focus on characters who might be identifiable because of some particular position or characteristic or relationship to the plot that the fictional character has.

5. Finally, Packager must see that all necessary and appropriate releases have been obtained.

In NBC's experience, it is often useful to obtain the services of an outside research entity, such as Fact or Fiction. These entities may spot problems of which the reviewing attorneys otherwise would not be aware . . .

Finally I am enclosing an Annotation Guide for use by the writer of the script for the program. Thank you for your cooperation. We look forward to working with you.

Very truly yours,

NBC Annotation Guide

Annotated scripts should contain for each script element—whether an event, setting, or segment of the dialogue—notes in the margin that provide the following information:

1. Whether the element presents or portrays:
   (a) Fact;
   (b) Fiction, but product of inference from fact; or
   (c) Fiction, not based on fact.
2. With regard to characters:
   (a) Whether the character is real, composite (of real individuals), or totally fictional.
   (b) Whether the character's name is real; and
   (c) Whether any corresponding real persons have signed releases.
3. Source material for the element;

(a) Book;
(b) Newspaper or magazine article;
(c) Recorded interview;
(d) Trial or deposition transcript;
(e) Any other source.

Source material identification should give the name of the source (for example, a *New York Times* article, with page reference and date). To the extent possible, identify multiple sources for each element. Retain copies of all materials, preferably cross-indexed by reference to script pages and scene numbers. Coding may be useful to avoid repeated lengthy references.

Descriptive annotation notes are helpful (for example, "setting is hotel suite because John Doe usually had business meetings in his hotel suite when visiting L.A.—*New York Times*; April 1, 2010, p. 8").

Appendix B: Marketability

In chapter 2, I touched very briefly on the marketplace for docudrama. In this appendix, I want to expand on one or two points raised in that section. Until now, we've been looking at the challenge of writing. However, at the end of the day, you want to sell your script and see that it gets made. This means knowing the marketplace, and knowing what the producers want and where to turn.

This means understanding moods, personalities, the instability of fashion, studios, international setups, and country quirks. It means trying to understand a process that is often highly irrational and always aggravating.

Sometimes, the successful suffer as much as novices in this process. Director Richard Attenborough made the rounds for almost twenty years before he could find a backer for *Gandhi*. This was because the marketplace seers knew there was no future for a film about a wizened, half-naked Indian politician who believed in nonviolence and was uninterested in sex. David Seidler had written successful scripts for Hollywood, but it still took him years to persuade backers that a film about a stuttering king could be successful.

So much for experts.

The marketing of scripts is a massive subject, and a great many books have been written about the subject. The two books I find most useful in this area are *Script Planning* by Tony Zaza, and *Selling a Screenplay,* by Sid Field. Both are good but say little on three background issues: changing fashions, codes and constraints, and the film market versus the TV market. A pity, because all three deserve attention.

Changing Fashions

The writer has to be aware of how and why fashions change. What was fine for yesterday maybe totally wrong for today. Hollywood practice is a good example.

Between 1927 and 1960, over 270 biopics were made in Hollywood by the major studios, with Producer Darryl Zanuck acting as the key arbitrator on taste. Under his lead, Warner Brothers and others turned out film after film idealizing the famed of history, from Zola and Disraeli to Alexander Graham Bell and Louis Pasteur. And when they ran out of statesmen and scientists, they turned to entertainers like Gershwin and Cohan, or sportsmen like Knute Rockne and Babe Ruth.

Today, there has been a major shift in biography. Lives are generally translated to the screen in a more serious and truthful fashion and are beginning to appear as theatrical features as often as they appear as TV biopics. Hence, the success of *The Queen, Nixon,* and *The Iron Lady.*

Though the "heroic" bio film is still around, the emphasis, at least on TV, has shifted away from stories of the famous to stories of ordinary people to whom unusual things have happened. In his book *Biopics,* George Custen puts it this way: "Notoriety has in some sense replaced noteworthiness as the proper frame for biography. The perennially famous have been replaced by the momentarily observed."

CODES AND CONSTRAINTS

Not only does the marketability of certain subjects change, but also the way they can be treated. From the 1930s through the 1950s, for example, Hollywood was constrained by the requirements of the production code. This code, originally set up by the producers themselves, imposed a prim morality on everything to do with screen behavior and language.

Today, the code no longer exists, but many of its restraints have entered television. Thus, while almost anything is possible on the big screen, such as Colin Firth shouting "shit, shit, shit" in *The King's Speech,* more caution has to be exercised when writing for television, maybe with the exception of HBO. Thus, the language, violence, and obscenity of a film such as *Reservoir Dogs* would not be acceptable in the normal television movie of the week. In other words, television says yes to sex and violence, but only within limits.

FILM OR TV MARKET

The problem of codes and constraints is really just one element of a larger question. What market should you choose, film or TV? Obviously, the feature film offers you larger rewards as a writer, but there are many other matters that have to be discussed.

It would be simple if the battle lines were clearly drawn, but they're not. *Barbarians at the Gate* cost $7 million to film and was originally commissioned by Columbia. Eventually, Columbia considered it too problematic for a theatrical audience, and it was taken over by HBO. Even among networks, there are differences as to what is suitable material for the screen. *And the Band Played On* was considered by NBC and then dropped because the subject of AIDS was seen as too uncongenial for a family audience. HBO had fewer qualms and went on to make one of the biggest successes of the TV season.

Where your subject crosses country boundaries, the increase in international TV coproductions offers quite a lot of scope for the writer. Thus, the signing of coproduction deals between the BBC and HBO, and between Granada TV and HBO, lead to a plethora of excellent docudramas such as the *Exxon Valdez* film, and *The Tragedy of Flight 103*. Again, when I was trying to launch *The First Fagin*, eventually my partners and I put together a deal with ZDF (Germany) and Screen Australia.

Looked at from a distance, there do seem to be a few tentative rules that will help you see whether your best bet is TV or a film feature.

TV seems best when your story is

Local or provincial;

Hot news that requires dramatizing while the story is still fresh in the public mind (such British TV's *Dr. Death*, which dealt with Harold Shipman's murder of fifteen of his patients and which was screened soon after the end of the trial; again, the dramatization of David Irving's prosecution against Deborah Lipstadt for libel, *The Holocaust on Trial*, was screened *four days* after the end of the trial; such speed and turn-around would have been impossible had these stories been done as features);

Is best done on a low budget;

Requires miniseries treatment such as *Band of Brothers*;

Is a "woman's movie."

This last proviso may seem strange until one realizes that TV has almost entirely co-opted the woman's movie of the 1940s, hence the large number of woman-centered docudramas.

Film seems best when your story

Is extremely visual, such as *Aviator* or *Amelia*

Is less tied to the headlines

Requires large budgets and big stars like Meryl Streep and Al Pacino

Is of epic quality like *A Bridge Too Far*

Has really universal appeal

Requires a long production time.

Index

Alan Rosenthal has made more than fifty films. He has taught film at Stanford University and the Hebrew University of Jerusalem, as well as in Britain, Australia, and Mexico; and his film awards include a Christopher and a Peabody, among others. His recent docudrama *The First Fagin*, about the transportation of convicts to Australia in the nineteenth century, was invited for special feature presentation at the Melbourne International Film Festival in 2012.